500

soups

500

soups

the only soup compendium you'll ever need

Susannah Blake

SELLERS
PUBLISHING

A Quintet Book

Published by Sellers Publishing, Inc.
161 John Roberts Road, South Portland, Maine 04106

For ordering information:
(800) 625-3386 Toll Free
(207) 772-6814 Fax

Visit our Web site: www.rsvp.com • E-mail: rsp@rsvp.com

ISBN-13: 978-1-56906-978-3
QUIN.FSO

This book was designed and produced by
Quintet Publishing Limited
6 Blundell Street
London N7 9BH

Library of Congress Control Number: 2007920053

Senior Editor: Ruth Patrick
Art Director: Dean Martin
Photography: Ian Garlick
Home Economist: Wendy Sweetser
Creative Director: Richard Dewing
Publisher: Gaynor Sermon

10 9 8 7 6 5

Manufactured in Singapore by Pica Digital Pte Ltd.
Printed in China by SNP Leefung Printers Ltd.

contents

introduction

For as long as humans have been cooking food over a fire, soup has been eaten in one form or another — from the earliest, most basic broths left over from simmering ingredients in a pot of water, or sophisticated concoctions specially created to be served and eaten on their own. Soup is made and eaten all over the world, from Italian *zuppa*, German *suppe,* and Balkan *ciorba* to Vietnamese *sup*, Persian *shorba*, and Central Asian *sorpa* or *shorpo*. They all share a common texture characteristic, in that they are all liquid dishes, usually served in bowls.

The bulk of soups are cooked — usually meat, poultry, fish, or vegetables simmered in stock — but you will also find uncooked soups, such as Spanish gazpacho and Middle Eastern-style yogurt soups, for which uncooked ingredients are blended together to make a smooth soup. Soups may be light and clear, such as broth or consommé, rich and creamy, thick and substantial, or chunky and stewlike. Although they are usually savory, there are also a few sweet soups, including those made with melon, cherry, or pear. Sweet soups are generally served in small quantities.

There are many types of soup and an almost infinite number of combinations of ingredients. The flavoring ingredients give each soup its own distinctive character. In their wonderful variety, soups can be eaten at almost any time of day, at any time of year. In Asia, they are often served for breakfast. Lighter soups made from vegetables can make a healthy snack between meals, or a more substantial soup can make a sustaining meal in a bowl. Soup is one of the classic first courses on Western menus, served before the main course. It is also perfect for a light lunch or even as a late-night snack before bed. In winter, soups can be fabulous warmers — warding off the seasonal chills — while in summer, chilled soups can be gloriously refreshing.

Wholesome and comforting, plain or complex, sophisticated or simple, whatever kind of soup you're looking for, you're sure to find it here. Packed with delicious recipes and inspiring serving suggestions, this compendium proves that there really is a soup for every occasion.

equipment

Making soups is very easy and requires very little specialty equipment.

measuring equipment: scales, measuring cups & spoons
Although most soup recipes are very easy and can be adapted according to the ingredients you have on hand, accurate measuring equipment will be invaluable.

chopping board & knives
Good knives and a board are essential for cutting vegetables, meat, poultry, fish, and shellfish. A serrated knife is useful for cutting bread to serve with soup.

vegetable peeler
A vegetable peeler is more practical and efficient than a knife for peeling firm vegetables and fruit such as apples and pears. A vegetable peeler is also a useful tool for paring or shaving fine slivers or slices from Parmesan cheese.

grater
Choose a grater with several different hole sizes for coarse and fine grating.

garlic press
Although you can crush garlic using the flat blade of a knife, a garlic press is useful and easy to use, particularly if you need to crush several cloves.

cooking pan
Choose a large, heavy pan with a lid that fits well. This is useful for all stages of cooking soups and for long-simmering stock.

wooden spoons

Useful for stirring ingredients when frying them in the first stages of a recipe, for stirring soup during cooking, and for stirring in ingredients at a later stage.

food processor or blender

To make smooth soups, you will usually need a food processor or a blender. There are several styles of blenders, including freestanding and handheld types. Handheld blenders are particularly useful for soup-making because they can be used directly in the pan, rather than pouring the soup into a food processor or blender, then returning it to the pan. Experiment with the settings on a food processor to achieve the best consistency — some processors do not reduce liquids to as smooth a texture as a blender. A food mill is useful for crushing and puréeing the cooked soup.

strainers

A strainer or sieve is useful for straining soup. There are several types, including a large fine-mesh wire strainer (for sieving food to a purée), a nylon mesh strainer for foods that discolor, and a colander for draining large ingredients.

potato masher

A masher can crush tender cooked vegetables to make a rough textured soup. This technique can be used to make chunky soups if you do not have a food processor or blender.

skimmer

A flat, round perforated utensil — or skimmer — is used to lift scum or froth from stock and soup. A slotted spoon will also do the job, or a large flat-bowled metal spoon can be used.

stocks

A good stock is the essential base for almost every soup. Good-quality stock is now available in supermarkets, delicatessens, and grocery stores, as cubes, bouillon powder, in long-life cartons, or fresh from the refrigerator. It is worth using good-quality stock as it will make all the difference to the flavor of soup. Homemade stock can be frozen, so it is a good idea to make a large batch and freeze it in smaller quantities, ready for thawing and using in recipes. Rigid cartons with good lids are practical for storing stock in the freezer.

vegetable stock

2 onions, roughly chopped
2 carrots, sliced
2 celery stalks, roughly chopped
1 bay leaf
2 sprigs fresh thyme

4 sprigs fresh parsley
1 tsp. black peppercorns
1/2 tsp. salt
6 3/4 cups water
Makes about 5 cups

Put all the ingredients in a saucepan, add the water, and bring to a boil. Reduce the heat and simmer for about 1 hour, skimming off any scum that rises to the surface. Strain the stock through a strainer and leave to cool, then chill or freeze until ready to use.

chicken stock

1 chicken carcass
2 onions, roughly chopped
2 carrots, sliced
2 celery stalks, roughly chopped

2 bay leaves
1 tsp. black peppercorns
1/2 tsp. salt
6 3/4 cups water
Makes about 5 cups

Put all the ingredients in a saucepan, add the water, and bring to a boil. Reduce the heat and simmer gently, skimming off the scum occasionally, for about 1 1/2 hours. Strain the stock through a strainer and leave to cool, then chill or freeze until ready to use.

beef stock

2 lb. beef bones
1 onion, roughly chopped
1 leek, roughly chopped
2 carrots, sliced
1 celery stalk, roughly chopped
1 bay leaf

2 sprigs fresh thyme
4 sprigs fresh parsley
1 tsp. black peppercorns
1/2 tsp. salt
6 3/4 cups (3 1/2 pints) water
Makes about 5 cups

Preheat the oven to 425°F (220°C). Put the bones in a roasting pan and roast for about 40 minutes. Transfer the bones to a large saucepan and add all the remaining ingredients. Bring to a boil, then reduce the heat and simmer, skimming off any scum occasionally, for about 3 hours. Strain the stock through a strainer and leave to cool, then chill or freeze until ready to use.

fish stock

1 lb. fish bones (without gills as they are bitter)
1 onion, roughly chopped
1 leek, roughly sliced
2 celery stalks, chopped
1 bay leaf

4 parsley stalks
1/2 tsp. black peppercorns
1/2 tsp. salt
5 1/4 cups water
Makes about 5 cups

Put the fish bones in a saucepan, add all the remaining ingredients. Bring to a boil, then reduce the heat and simmer gently, skimming off any scum occasionally, for about 30 minutes. Strain the stock through a strainer and leave to cool completely, then chill or freeze until ready to use.

serving soup

There are hundreds of different ways to serve soup, including when and how to present it. Soup can be served on its own, simply ladled into a bowl, or accompaniments, garnishes, and toppings can be added to transform a plain soup into something extraordinary. Even if you don't have the time to make a pot of soup, you can transform a bowl of ready-made soup; try some of the following suggestions.

accompaniments

Chunks, wedges, or slices of bread are probably the simplest of all accompaniments. There is plenty of choice, including bought or homemade.

Heat or warm a loaf of bread in the oven while the soup cooks. This is a clever choice as it gives the impression that the bread is freshly baked with none of the effort of making a loaf at the same time as preparing soup.

Try different types of bread, including crusty baguettes and whole-grain loaves; Italian ciabatta and flavored focaccia; wholesome rye breads (such as pumpernickel), and individual rolls. More unusual choices include biscuits, wedges of warm naan bread, or pita bread. You may want to serve the bread plain, or with butter for spreading.

Bread can be plain or toasted. Small slices of toasted bread, such as baguette, ciabatta, or brioche, can be topped to make bruschetta or crostini. These delicious accompaniments can be served on the side or floated on top of the soup as a sophisticated garnish. Garlic bread is another great accompaniment that can be made simply by splitting a baguette or ciabatta, spreading the slices with garlic butter, wrapping in foil, and heating in the oven until hot and crisp.

A cheeseboard, perhaps with a small selection of cheese and some grapes or celery, is an excellent choice for complementing the soup and bread, and making a delicious light, but satisfying, meal.

garnishes

One of the joys of serving soup is the wide choice of garnishes that can be added so easily just before serving. From a sprinkling of herbs, a swirl of cream to crispy croutons, tangy salsas, crispy shallots, or even a couple of ice cubes for a chilled soup. Whatever you choose, with a little care, it can transform a simple bowl of soup into a gourmet treat. Garnishes should add flavor and texture, and the visual appeal that is so important for whetting the appetite and stimulating the taste buds.

croutons

These crisp cubes of toasted or fried bread are a classic topping for soups, bringing crunchy texture contrast. The simplest croutons are made from cubes of bread, fried in olive oil or butter until crisp, then drained on paper towels, and left to cool. You can make big, chunky croutons out of thick slices. Throw a little crushed garlic into the pan for the last minute of cooking. Cubes or wedges of toasted naan bread, ciabatta, or focaccia also make good crouton-type toppings for soup.

bruschetta & crostini

Slices of baguette or ciabatta, brushed with oil, then broiled until crisp and golden, are perfect with soup, either as a chunky garnish or an accompaniment instead of bread. For hearty soups, they are a good alternative to mini croutons — make them plain, or rub one side with a cut clove of garlic. Drizzle with more oil and sprinkle with herbs and ground black pepper, or top with seeded, chopped tomatoes, or a spoonful or two of salsa. Another option is to spread them with pesto and top with charbroiled vegetables; or add a dollop of sour cream, or mayo, on to bite-size crostini, and top with a twist of smoked salmon or salami. The options are endless, so let your imagination go wild.

vegetable chips

Great for serving on the side, a handful of potato or vegetable chips are a simple alternative to crispy croutons. Try sweet potato, beet, and carrot chips for color and sweet flavor. Experiment with traditional types, very fine chips and thick-cut types. Just scatter a handful on top of the soup just before serving.

fresh herbs

For color, flavor, and aroma, fresh herbs are an easy and delicious choice when it comes to finishing soups. Snipped chives or a sprinkling of chopped parsley, mint, or sage look and taste fabulous. Fine cutting is important for firm-textured herbs, but soft leaves can be left whole, or torn. Some herbs are good finely shredded — sage leaves, for example, can be rolled and cut into very fine shreds. Torn basil leaves, or whole leaves, or sprigs of herbs, such as thyme or oregano, all look lovely sprinkled over soup just before serving. Herb flowers are a great choice when in season and they look especially pretty on delicate, special-occasion soups or pale-colored cream soups.

chili

Spicy soups look lively when garnished with sliced, diced, or slivered chilies, but be sure to seed them and remove the white pith inside as this is where the heat resides.

scallions

Fresh scallions, very thinly sliced or shredded, look good and they add fresh color and punchy flavor. They are traditional and excellent with Asian-style soups and broths, but also work well sprinkled on a wide variety of other soups, such as simple tomato soup, for extra taste and texture.

onion rings
Wafer-thin slices of raw onion, divided into rings, can look appetizing and they bring a twist of flavor to subdued soups. Red onions are a good choice for their color and mild flavor; white onions or mild Bermuda onions are also delicious.

salad vegetables
Finely diced cucumber, bell peppers, and tomatoes make good-looking garnishes, particularly on summer soups. Just use one, or toss a few different vegetables together with herbs and a drizzle of olive oil, red wine vinegar, and seasoning, then spoon on top of the soup.

citrus fruits
Grated lemon, orange, or lime rind look fresh and add a particularly distinctive zesty flavor that cannot be achieved by using juice alone. Finely grated citrus rind is also delicious sprinkled on simple bruschetta after broiling.

seeds
Toasted seeds, such as sesame, pumpkin, and sunflower, go well with soup. Not only do they look appetizing and add a wonderful texture and color, they are also a healthy option. Try them in place of croutons and combine them with finely chopped herbs.

ice cubes
Perfect for finishing chilled soups, a few cubes of ice bobbing in a bowl add a certain sophistication, keeping the soup chilled on a hot day. Add them just before serving.

toppings

Toppings are perfect for spooning, swirling, or floating. Cream, yogurt, flavored oils, dressings or relishes are all suitable — experiment with textures and flavors to complement the soup they are dressing. When selecting a topping, think about the main ingredients in the soup, how substantial they are, and whether they would benefit from being enriched by a complementary refreshing topping.

yogurt

A low-fat alternative to cream, yogurt works particularly well spooned or swirled on top of Indian-style spiced soups. For swirling or drizzling, select thin yogurt or thin down the thicker types, such as strained Greek-style yogurt, by stirring in a little milk.

cream

Pale cream contrasts with richly colored soup. Creams are particularly good for topping smooth, blended soups. Light or heavy cream can be drizzled or swirled into soup just before serving; thick creams, such as crème fraîche and sour cream, are added in dollops. Cream enriches the flavor of the soup, at the same time taking the edge off punchy ingredients — making them more mellow.

pesto

Richly flavored pesto looks good and adds flavor. It works particularly well with Mediterranean-style soups and vegetable soups. It can be used plain or blended with a little extra-virgin olive oil for finer drizzling. Homemade classic pesto, with fresh basil, garlic, pine nuts, Parmesan cheese, and olive oil, bursts with flavor and bright green color. When selecting storebought pesto, go for a good-quality product. There are many variations on the traditional classic paste, including pesto with bell peppers, tomatoes, herbs other than basil, different nuts, and various oils.

salsas, relishes & chutneys

These can be spooned on top of soups to give an extra zing. Make your own or buy good-quality products. These can be chunky or fairly smooth, piquant, mild, or hot and spicy. Instead of spooning them straight on the soup, try topping toasted, finely sliced bread or slightly larger croutons.

fish, ham & bacon

Strips of smoked salmon or flakes of smoked fish can make a stunning finishing touch scattered on the surface of soup just before serving. A small spoonful of caviar, perhaps paired with a dollop of sour cream, looks and tastes terrific. Wafer-thin strips of prosciutto can be used in the same way. For a crisp topping, try broiling a couple of slices of bacon until crisp, then snip them into pieces, and scatter over the soup.

cheese

Try scattering shredded hard cheese on top of a hearty vegetable soup, or top with shavings of Parmesan cheese. Crumbly cheeses, such as blue cheese or feta, are also perfect for sprinkling. Creamy cheeses, such as Gorgonzola or goat cheese, can be cut into small cubes and sprinkled on top. The cheese melts with the heat of soup, producing a lovely texture and enriching the flavor.

omelets

Thin omelets are perfect for topping broths or lightly thickened soups. They should be well flavored and finely cut, either by rolling, slicing, and shaking out into thin shreds, or cut into small shapes using cocktail cutters. Neatly diced omelet, cut into strips and then across, is also good on soup. Herbs, spices, and/or finely chopped vegetables, such as scallions, bell peppers, and tomatoes, are good cooked in the omelet.

cooled & chilled

When it's hot and sunny outside, nothing quite
beats a bowl of lusciously flavored, ice-cold soup.
Chilled soups make the perfect choice for a simple,
yet sophisticated, appetizer, so prepare one of these
superlative recipes for a special dinner.

iced carrot & orange soup

see variations page 38

This fresh, zesty soup makes a delicious appetizer, or refreshingly light summer lunch served with chunks of crusty bread.

2 tbsp. olive oil
1 onion, chopped
1 lb. carrots, sliced
1 small potato, chopped

5 cups vegetable stock
Juice of 2 oranges
Salt and ground black pepper
Ice cubes and chopped fresh mint, to garnish

Heat the oil in a large saucepan. Add the onion and cook gently for about 5 minutes. Stir in the carrots and potato, and add the stock. Bring to a boil, then reduce the heat, and cover the pan. Simmer for about 20 minutes, until the vegetables are tender.

Purée the soup in a blender until smooth. Pour the soup into a large bowl, cover, and leave to cool. Stir in the orange juice and chill the soup for at least 2 hours.

Check the seasoning, adding salt and pepper to taste, and ladle the soup in bowls. Add a couple of ice cubes to each bowl of soup, and sprinkle with chopped fresh mint.

Serves 4

chilled avocado soup with fiery tomato salsa

see variations page 39

Smooth, creamy, and incredibly quick to make, this luscious soup is perfect for a quick lunch or dinner.

2 large ripe avocados
1 red chili, seeded and chopped
1 garlic clove, chopped
5 cups chicken stock, chilled
Juice of 1 lime
Salt and ground black pepper
Ice cubes, to serve

for the salsa

2 ripe tomatoes, seeded and finely chopped
2 scallions, sliced
1 green chili, seeded and finely chopped
2 tbsp. chopped fresh cilantro
Juice of 1/2 lime

First make the salsa. Combine the tomatoes, scallions, chili, and cilantro in a small bowl. Season with a little salt, add the lime juice, and stir until the ingredients are thoroughly combined. Cover and set aside.

To make the soup, halve and pit the avocados, then scoop the flesh into a food processor or blender. Add the chili, garlic, and stock, and process until smooth. Add the lime juice and season to taste with salt and pepper, then process briefly to mix.

Pour the soup into bowls. Top with ice cubes and a spoonful of salsa. Serve immediately.

Serves 4

vichyssoise

see variations page 40

This classic chilled soup is perfect for an al fresco lunch on a hot summer's day or as an elegant appetizer before a special meal.

2 tbsp. (1/4 stick) butter
3 leeks, sliced
1 medium-large potato, chopped
3 1/2 cups vegetable stock

1 1/2 cups milk, plus extra to finish
Generous 1/2 cup light cream
Salt and ground black pepper
Snipped chives and croutons, to garnish

Melt the butter in a large saucepan. Add the leeks, stir, and cook gently for about 5 minutes, until softened. Add the potato and stock, and bring to a boil. Reduce the heat, cover, and simmer for about 15 minutes, until the potato is tender.

Process the soup in a food processor or blender until smooth. Stir in the milk and cream, and season to taste with salt and pepper. Leave to cool, then chill for at least 2 hours.

To serve, taste and add more salt and pepper if necessary. Add a splash more milk if the soup is slightly too thick, then ladle it into bowls. Sprinkle each portion with chives and croutons, and serve immediately.

Serves 4

simple spanish gazpacho

see variations page 41

The secret to getting a really good flavor when making this classic Spanish soup is to use good-quality, ripe ingredients, particularly the tomatoes.

2 lb. ripe tomatoes, peeled, seeded, and roughly chopped
1 cucumber, peeled and roughly chopped
1 red bell pepper, seeded and roughly chopped
1 red onion, roughly chopped
2 garlic cloves, crushed
5 tbsp. olive oil
About 1 1/3 cups cold water

3 slices dry (stale) bread, crusts removed and cut into chunks
2 tbsp. sherry vinegar
Pinch of sugar
Salt and ground black pepper
Finely diced red onion, cucumber, and fresh basil leaves, to garnish

Put the tomatoes, cucumber, pepper, onion, and garlic in a food processor. Add the olive oil. Pour in about half the water and place the bread on top. Process until thick and smooth.

Transfer the soup to a large bowl. Stir in most of the remaining water, vinegar, sugar, and salt and pepper to taste. Chill for at least 2 hours.

To serve, check the consistency and add a splash more water if necessary. Ladle the soup into bowls. Garnish with onion, cucumber, and a few basil leaves, and serve.

Serves 4

cucumber & yogurt soup

see variations page 42

Popular in the Middle East, this simple, quick, and refreshing soup is perfect in summer, either as an appetizer or for a light lunch.

3 cucumbers, seeded and roughly chopped
1 1/2 cups Greek yogurt
1 cup vegetable stock, chilled
2 tbsp. chopped fresh mint, plus extra
   to garnish

Salt and ground black pepper
Paprika, for sprinkling
4 scallions, cut into short lengths and
   finely shredded

Purée the cucumbers in a food processor or blender until smooth. Add the yogurt and stock, and pulse briefly to combine.

Pour the soup into a large bowl. Stir in the mint and add salt and pepper to taste, then chill for at least 2 hours, or until ready to serve.

Ladle the soup into bowls. Sprinkle each portion with mint, a pinch of paprika, and scallions, and serve.

Serves 4

chilled tomato & basil soup with tomato sorbet

see variations page 43

This light, elegant soup makes a stylish appetizer before a special meal. It is particularly good in summer when tomatoes are ripe and basil plentiful.

2 tbsp. olive oil
1 onion, chopped
2 garlic cloves, crushed
1 lb. (approx.) tomatoes, peeled and chopped
1/2 tsp. brown sugar
5 cups vegetable or chicken stock
Handful of fresh basil
Salt and ground black pepper

for the tomato sorbet

1 lb. (approx.) tomatoes, peeled and seeded
1/4 fresh red chili, seeded and chopped
1/2 garlic clove, crushed
1 tsp. brown sugar
1/4 tsp. balsamic vinegar
Handful of fresh basil, plus extra to garnish

For the sorbet, purée the tomatoes, chili, garlic, sugar, vinegar, and basil in a food processor. Add salt and pepper to taste and chill. Churn in an ice cream-maker or freeze in a suitable container (3 to 8 hours), processing twice in a food processor to break up the ice crystals.

Heat the oil in a large saucepan. Add the onion and garlic, and cook gently for 5 minutes. Add the tomatoes, sugar, and stock. Bring to a boil, then simmer, covered, for 20 minutes. Cool, blend until smooth, adding the basil, and chill for at least 2 hours. Place a scoop of sorbet in each bowl. Ladle in the soup, garnish with a few basil leaves, and serve immediately.

Serves 4

sweet pea & mint soup

see variations page 44

This lovely, fresh, green soup is incredibly simple to make in less than 15 minutes.

2 tbsp. olive oil
4 shallots, chopped
2 garlic cloves, crushed
2 1/4 lb. (8 cups) frozen peas
5 cups vegetable or chicken stock

1 tbsp. chopped fresh mint, plus extra
   to garnish
Salt and ground black pepper
1/2 cup heavy cream

Heat the oil in a large saucepan. Add the shallots and garlic, and cook gently for about 2 minutes. Stir in the peas and vegetable stock. Bring to a boil, then remove from the heat.

Process the soup in a blender or food processor until smooth. Stir in the mint and salt and pepper to taste. Leave the soup to cool and then chill it for at least 2 hours before serving.

Check the consistency of the soup and stir in a splash of water, if necessary. Pour the soup into bowls or glasses. Swirl in the cream and serve sprinkled with more fresh mint.

Serves 4

chilled sorrel soup

see variations page 45

Fresh sorrel comes into season in spring. It has an intense and sharp, lemonlike flavor.

1 small potato, diced
3 3/4 cups vegetable stock
Bunch of scallions, shredded
1 lb. sorrel, roughly shredded

3/4 cup white wine
1/2 cup heavy cream
Salt and ground black pepper
Snipped chives, to garnish

Put the potato and stock in a large saucepan. Bring to a boil, reduce the heat, cover, and simmer for about 15 minutes, until the potato is tender.

Stir in the scallions and three-quarters of the sorrel. Process the soup in a food processor or blender until smooth. Pour the soup into a large bowl. Stir in the wine, cream, remaining sorrel, and salt and pepper to taste. Let cool, cover, then chill the soup for at least 2 hours before serving.

Ladle the soup into bowls and sprinkle with snipped chives, then serve immediately.

Serves 4

beet & orange soup with sour cream

see variations page 46

This sweet, fragrant, ruby red soup makes a stunning appetizer. It is refreshing for a summer lunch or uplifting at any time of the year.

2 tbsp. olive oil
1 onion, chopped
1 1/2 lb. raw beets, peeled and chopped
5 cups vegetable or chicken stock
1/2 tsp. grated orange zest
Juice of 2 oranges

Salt and ground black pepper
1 1/2 tbsp. sour cream
4 mini blinis
Snipped fresh chives and grated orange zest,
    for sprinkling

Heat the oil in a large saucepan. Add the onion and cook gently for about 5 minutes. Add the beets and stock, stir, and bring to a boil. Reduce the heat, cover, and simmer for about 20 minutes, until the beets are tender.

Process the soup in a food processor or blender until smooth. Pour into a large bowl and leave to cool. Stir in the orange zest, juice, and salt and pepper to taste. Chill the soup for at least 2 hours.

To serve, spoon a small dollop of sour cream on each blini and sprinkle with orange zest, and chives. Ladle the soup into serving bowls and float a blini on each portion.

Serves 4

lettuce & scallion soup

see variations page 47

This light and simple soup makes a refreshing appetizer on a hot day.

2 tbsp. olive oil
1 onion, chopped
2 garlic cloves, crushed
4 1/4 cups vegetable or chicken stock
4 heads bibb lettuce, shredded
2 bunches scallions, sliced

1/2 cup dry white wine
Salt and ground black pepper
3 tbsp. mayonnaise
1/2 tsp. harissa (hot chili paste)
4 slices baguette
Chopped fresh parsley, for sprinkling

Heat the oil in a large saucepan. Add the onion and garlic, and cook gently for 5 minutes. Pour in the stock and bring to a boil. Stir in the lettuce and scallions, and cook for about 1 minute, then remove from the heat.

Process the soup in a food processor or blender until smooth. Pour the soup into a large bowl. Stir in the wine and add salt and pepper to taste. Leave the soup to cool, then chill it for at least 2 hours.

To serve, combine the mayonnaise and harissa. Toast the baguette slices on both sides until golden and top with mayonnaise and a sprinkling of parsley. Ladle the soup into serving bowls and float a toast on each portion. Serve immediately.

Serves 4

variations

iced carrot & orange soup

see base recipe page 19

iced carrot, tomato & orange soup
Prepare the basic recipe, adding 3 peeled, chopped tomatoes with the carrots.

iced carrot, pepper & orange soup
Prepare the basic recipe, adding 2 seeded, chopped red bell peppers with the carrots.

creamy iced carrot & orange soup
Prepare the basic recipe, stirring 3 tablespoons mascarpone into the blended soup before cooling and chilling. Serve topped with a swirl of cream.

iced carrot, orange & cilantro soup
Prepare the basic recipe, stirring 2 tablespoons chopped fresh cilantro into the cooled soup. Serve sprinkled with more cilantro in place of the mint.

iced carrot, leek & orange soup
Prepare the basic recipe, using 1 sliced leek in place of the onion.

variations

chilled avocado soup with fiery tomato salsa

see base recipe page 21

chilled avocado soup with fiery tomato salsa toasts

Prepare the basic recipe and pour the soup into bowls but don't use the salsa. Toast 8 slices of baguette on both sides until golden, then top with the salsa, and drizzle with a little olive oil. Serve immediately, with the soup, garnished with ice cubes.

chilled avocado soup with fiery tomato salsa & sour cream

Prepare the basic recipe. Serve the soup topped with a dollop of sour cream as well as the salsa and ice.

chilled avocado soup with fiery tomato salsa & crunchy tortillas

Prepare the basic recipe. Do not add ice cubes but top each bowl of soup with tortilla chips. Serve the salsa separately with more tortilla chips.

hot avocado soup with fiery tomato salsa

Prepare the basic recipe. Pour the soup into a saucepan and heat it gently until almost simmering. Serve in bowls, topped with the salsa but omitting the ice cubes.

variations

vichyssoise

see base recipe page 22

vichyssoise with garlic & chive toasts
Prepare the basic recipe. Blend 1/4 cup (1/2 stick) butter with 1 crushed garlic clove, 2 tablespoons snipped chives, and a good grinding of black pepper. Toast 8 slices of baguette on both sides until golden, then spread with the butter, and serve with the soup.

extra-creamy vichyssoise
Prepare the basic recipe and serve each bowl topped with a generous swirl of cream before adding the chives and croutons.

vichyssoise with fresh mint
Prepare the basic recipe and serve sprinkled with chopped fresh mint in place of the chives.

leek & potato soup
Prepare the basic recipe. Return the puréed soup to the rinsed-out pan and stir in the milk and cream. Reheat, stirring often, until almost boiling. Ladle into bowls, sprinkle with chives and croutons, and serve.

simple spanish gazpacho

see base recipe page 25

simple spanish gazpacho with crispy croutons

Prepare the basic recipe. Cut 3 slices of crustless bread into cubes. Fry in
2 tablespoons olive oil until golden. Drain on paper towels and sprinkle
over the soup. (Omit the onion, cucumber, and basil garnish, if preferred.)

classic gazpacho

Prepare the basic recipe, omitting the garnish. Prepare croutons as in the
above variation. Finely dice 1 small red onion, 1 green bell pepper, and
1 small cucumber. Sprinkle the diced vegetables and croutons over the soup.

fragrant simple spanish gazpacho

Prepare the basic recipe, adding a handful of basil leaves before blending.

simple spanish gazpacho with garlic toasts

Prepare the basic recipe. Toast 4 to 8 slices of rustic sourdough bread. Rub
with a cut clove of garlic, then drizzle with olive oil. Serve with the soup.

simple spanish gazpacho with chorizo

Prepare the basic recipe. Fry slices of thinly sliced chorizo in a little olive
oil until crisp, then serve sprinkled over the soup, with or without the
basic garnish.

variations

cucumber & yogurt soup

see base recipe page 26

cucumber & yogurt soup with pita toasts

Prepare the basic recipe. To serve, toast 2 pita breads, then split them into two layers and cut into wedges. Place, toasted sides down, on the broiler pan and sprinkle with a little chopped garlic, and a drizzle of olive oil. Toast until golden. Sprinkle with chopped fresh parsley and serve with the soup.

cucumber & yogurt soup with herbs

Prepare the basic recipe, reducing the mint to 1 tablespoon and adding 1 tablespoon snipped fresh chives, and 1 tablespoon chopped fresh parsley. Sprinkle with more chopped fresh herbs before serving.

cucumber & yogurt soup with red bell pepper

Prepare the basic recipe. Seed and finely dice 1 small cucumber and 1 red bell pepper, and sprinkle over the soup with the scallions and mint.

cucumber & yogurt soup with lemon

Prepare the basic recipe, adding the grated zest of 1 lemon with the yogurt and stock.

chilled tomato & basil soup with tomato sorbet

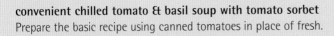

see base recipe page 29

convenient chilled tomato & basil soup with tomato sorbet
Prepare the basic recipe using canned tomatoes in place of fresh.

cream of tomato & basil soup
Prepare the basic soup recipe, but not the sorbet. Return the blended soup
to the saucepan and stir in 1/2 cup heavy cream. Heat through without
boiling, and serve topped with a swirl of cream.

chilled tomato & mint soup with tomato sorbet
Prepare the basic recipe, using mint in place of the basil.

chilled tomato & herb soup with tomato sorbet
Prepare the basic recipe, stirring in 2 tablespoons snipped fresh chives,
1 tablespoon chopped fresh mint, and 1 tablespoon chopped fresh parsley
into the chilled soup.

variations

sweet pea & mint soup

see base recipe page 30

sweet pea & mint soup with prosciutto

Prepare the basic recipe. Sprinkle each bowl of soup with bite-size strips of prosciutto before serving.

sweet pea & mint soup with crispy bacon

Prepare the basic recipe. Broil 2–3 bacon slices until crisp, then cut them into bite-size pieces. Sprinkle over the soup to serve.

sweet pea & mint soup with smoked salmon

Prepare the basic recipe. Sprinkle each bowl of soup with strips of smoked salmon to serve.

piping hot sweet pea & mint soup

Prepare the basic recipe and purée it freshly cooked. Reheat briefly if necessary, but do not overcook, and serve swirled with cream.

low-fat sweet pea & mint soup

Prepare the basic recipe, omitting the cream.

variations

chilled sorrel soup

see base recipe page 33

chilled sorrel & spinach soup
Prepare the basic recipe, adding 2 generous handfuls baby spinach leaves
with the first batch of sorrel.

iced sorrel soup
Float a few ice cubes in each bowl of soup before serving.

chilled spring leaf soup
Prepare the basic recipe, adding a generous handful of baby spinach leaves
and a handful of arugula leaves with the sorrel.

chilled sorrel & chive soup
Prepare the basic recipe. Stir in 2 tablespoons snipped fresh chives before
chilling. Serve sprinkled with more chives.

variations

beet & orange soup with sour cream

see base recipe page 34

chunky beet & orange soup with sour cream

Prepare the basic recipe, using finely chopped beets. Process half the cooked soup, then return it to the pan. Stir in the orange zest and juice, and serve hot, topped with the blinis.

beet & orange soup with vodka & sour cream

Prepare the basic recipe, stirring in 1/4 cup vodka just before serving.

quick beet & orange soup with sour cream

Prepare the basic recipe, using cooked beets in place of raw. Fry the onion, then add the beets and chilled stock. Blend without simmering first.

spiced beet & orange soup with sour cream

Prepare the basic recipe, adding 2 teaspoons ground coriander to the onion before stirring in the beets and stock.

variations

lettuce & scallion soup

see base recipe page 37

lettuce, pea & scallion soup
Prepare the basic recipe, adding 2 cups frozen peas with the stock.

lettuce, asparagus & scallion soup
Prepare the basic recipe, adding 1 bunch trimmed, sliced asparagus with the stock. Simmer the soup for about 3 minutes before adding the lettuce and scallions.

lettuce, spinach & scallion soup
Prepare the basic recipe, adding 2 large handfuls of spinach with the lettuce.

lettuce & scallion soup with lemon
Prepare the basic recipe. Stir 1 teaspoon grated lemon zest into the cooled soup before serving.

healthy &
wholesome

Soup is a great choice when you're looking for

a meal that will sustain and nourish. Low in fat

and packed with fresh, nutritious ingredients and

slow-release carbs, the soups in this chapter are all

designed to give your body the health kick it needs.

chicken noodle soup

see variations page 68

This comforting, wholesome, homemade soup is an old-fashioned cure-all — ideal when you're nursing a cold, or just to lift your spirits.

2 chicken leg portions (about 1 lb.), skinned
1 onion, quartered
3 celery stalks, sliced
1 large carrot, sliced
1 bay leaf

Small bunch of fresh parsley, plus handful
of flatleaf parsley leaves to serve
6 2/3 cups cold water
Salt and ground black pepper
4 oz angel hair pasta or vermicelli

Put the chicken, onion, celery, carrot, bay leaf, and bunch of parsley in a large saucepan. Add the cold water. Add about 3/4 teaspoon salt and a good grinding of black pepper, and bring to a boil. Reduce the heat, cover, and simmer the soup for about 20 minutes, or until the chicken is cooked.

Remove the chicken, strip off the meat, and set it aside. Return the bones to the pan. Cover and simmer for a further 1 1/2 hours. Meanwhile, cut the chicken into small pieces.

Strain the stock into a clean saucepan and bring it back to a boil. Break the noodles into pieces, add them to the stock, and simmer for 5 minutes, until tender. Stir in the chicken pieces and heat it through. Stir in the parsley leaves and serve.

Serves 4

spiced lentil, chickpea & chorizo soup

see variations page 69

This chunky, wholesome soup is packed with fiber and complex carbohydrates offering slow-release energy to keep you going for longer.

1/2 cup Puy lentils, or brown
   or green lentils
2 tbsp. olive oil
2 oz. chorizo, chopped
1 onion, finely chopped
2 garlic cloves, crushed
3 tsp. ground cumin
2 tsp. ground coriander

1/2 tsp. ground cinnamon
1/4 tsp. crushed dried chili pepper
4 tomatoes, peeled, seeded, and chopped
14-oz. can chickpeas, rinsed and drained
1 tbsp. tomato paste
5 cups vegetable or chicken stock
Salt and ground black pepper
Juice of about 1/2 lemon, to taste

Put the lentils in a large saucepan, pour in enough boiling water to cover them generously, and simmer for about 20 minutes, until just tender. Drain well.

Heat the oil in the rinsed-out saucepan and gently fry the chorizo, onion, and garlic for 4 minutes. Stir in the cumin, coriander, cinnamon, and chili, followed by the tomatoes, chickpeas, tomato paste, and stock. Bring to a boil, reduce the heat, cover, and simmer for 15 minutes. Add salt and pepper and lemon juice to taste. Ladle the soup into bowls and serve.

Serves 4

carrot, leek & potato soup

see variations page 70

This thick, warming soup is fat-free (depending on the stock used) so it makes a healthy, as well as filling, meal for those following a low-fat diet.

3 carrots, roughly chopped
2 leeks, sliced
1 small potato, roughly chopped
5 cups vegetable or chicken stock

Salt and ground black pepper
Chopped fresh parsley, to garnish (optional)
Crusty whole-grain bread, to serve

Put the carrots, leeks, and potato in a large saucepan. Pour in the stock and bring to a boil. Reduce the heat and simmer for about 20 minutes, until the vegetables are tender.

Process the soup in a food processor or blender until smooth. Add salt and pepper to taste, then pour the soup into serving bowls. Sprinkle with parsley, if desired, and serve with chunks of crusty whole-grain bread.

Serves 4

sweet-and-sour red cabbage soup with bacon

see variations page 71

This richly colored, robust, sweet-and-sour soup makes a perfect winter warmer. Serve with thick slices of crusty bread and a sharp cheddar cheese.

1 tbsp. olive oil
3 fatty bacon slices, snipped into
    bite-size pieces
2 onions, finely chopped
1/2 red cabbage, shredded
1 apple, peeled, cored, and finely chopped
2 tbsp. cider vinegar

2 tbsp. brown sugar
4 juniper berries, crushed
2 cloves
1/4 tsp. grated nutmeg
5 cups vegetable stock
Salt and ground black pepper

Heat the oil in a large saucepan. Add the bacon and onions, and cook gently for 5 minutes.

Add the cabbage, apple, vinegar, sugar, juniper berries, cloves, and nutmeg. Pour in the stock and stir well. Bring to a boil, reduce the heat, and cover the pan. Simmer the soup for about 20 minutes until the cabbage is tender.

Add salt and pepper to taste before serving.

Serves 4

ribollita

see variations page 72

This classic Italian soup is hearty and substantial. It is full of fiber and the vegetable goodness of cabbage, tomatoes, and beans.

2 tbsp. olive oil
1 onion, finely chopped
2 garlic cloves, crushed
14-oz. can chopped tomatoes
1 tbsp. tomato paste

5 cups vegetable or chicken stock
14-oz. can cannellini beans, drained
   and rinsed
8 oz. Savoy cabbage, shredded
Salt and ground black pepper

Heat the oil in a large saucepan. Add the onion and garlic, and cook gently for about 4 minutes. Add the tomatoes, tomato paste, stock, and beans. Stir well, then bring to a boil. Reduce the heat and simmer gently for about 20 minutes.

Transfer about half of the beans and vegetables to a food processor, and add a couple of ladlefuls of the stock. Process to a smooth purée, then stir the purée back into the soup.

Add the cabbage, bring back to a boil, and reduce the heat. Simmer for 5 to 10 minutes, until the cabbage is tender. Add salt and pepper to taste and serve.

Serves 4

green bean soup with tuna & tapenade toasts

see variations page 73

This chunky vegetable soup, packed with green beans, is inspired by the classic Niçoise salad. Any leftover tapenade can be stored in the refrigerator for another use.

2 tbsp. olive oil, plus extra for brushing
1 onion, finely chopped
2 garlic cloves, crushed
4 ripe tomatoes, peeled and chopped
4 1/4 cups vegetable stock
1 large potato, finely diced
8 oz. green beans, cut into 1-in. lengths
Salt and ground black pepper
4 oz. tuna steak

4 slices baguette
1 hard-cooked egg, quartered

for the tapenade

1 cup pitted black olives
1 garlic clove, crushed
2 anchovies
1 tsp. capers, rinsed and drained
2 tbsp. olive oil

Heat the oil in a large saucepan and cook the onion and garlic for 5 minutes. Add the tomatoes and stock. Boil, reduce the heat, cover and simmer for 10 minutes. Add the potato and cook for 5 minutes, then the beans, and cook for another 3 minutes. Add salt and pepper to taste. For the tapenade, purée all the ingredients in a food processor. Season with pepper. Brush the tuna with oil, and season with salt and pepper. Heat a nonstick skillet, sear the tuna for 1 to 2 minutes each side, then slice into thick strips. Toast the baguette slices, spread with tapenade, and top with tuna and egg. Ladle the soup into bowls and add the toasts.

Serves 4

black bean soup with sour cream

see variations page 74

This thick, nourishing soup makes a healthy lunch or dinner dish.

1 1/2 cups dried black beans, soaked overnight
   in cold water
2 tbsp. olive oil
1 onion, chopped
3 garlic cloves, crushed
1/4 tsp. crushed dried chili
2 tsp. ground cumin

1 tsp. ground coriander
5 cups vegetable or chicken stock
Juice of about 2 limes, to taste
Salt and ground black pepper
5 tbsp. sour cream
Chopped fresh cilantro, to garnish

Drain the beans and put in a large saucepan. Pour in boiling water to cover generously and boil rapidly for 10 minutes, skimming off any scum that rises to the surface. Reduce the heat, cover, and simmer for about 1 hour, until the beans are tender. Drain.

Heat the oil in the rinsed-out saucepan. Add the onion and garlic, and cook gently for about 5 minutes. Stir in the chili, cumin, and coriander, followed by the beans and stock. Bring to a boil. Reduce the heat, cover, and simmer gently for about 10 minutes.

Process the soup in a food processor or blender until smooth. Stir in lime juice and salt and pepper to taste. Ladle the soup into bowls, top with sour cream, and garnish with cilantro.

Serves 4

beef & barley soup

see variations page 75

This chunky soup offers everything you need in a meal — protein, carbohydrates, and fresh vegetables cooked until just tender.

2 tbsp. olive oil
1 lb. lean tender steak, cubed
1 onion, finely chopped
2 garlic cloves, crushed
1/2 cup pearled barley
5 1/2 cups beef stock

1 tsp. fresh thyme leaves
3 carrots, chopped
3 celery stalks, sliced
1 large potato, diced
Salt and ground black pepper

Heat the oil in a large nonstick saucepan. Add the beef and cook quickly until browned all over. Use a draining spoon to transfer the meat to a plate and set aside. Add the onion and garlic to the pan, and fry gently for about 4 minutes, then add the barley, stock, and thyme. Return the beef to the pan.

Bring to the boil, reduce the heat, cover, and simmer for about 45 minutes. Add the carrots, celery, and potato, and simmer for a further 15 minutes, until the meat and vegetables are tender. Season the soup to taste, then ladle it into bowls and serve.

Serves 4

mediterranean vegetable soup

see variations page 76

This rich tomato broth is spiked with capers to make a wonderfully healthy, light soup for summer and early fall when these vegetables are at their best.

2 tbsp. olive oil
1 onion, finely chopped
2 garlic cloves, crushed
4 large ripe tomatoes, peeled and chopped
1 red bell pepper, seeded and finely chopped
1 tbsp. sun-dried tomato paste

5 cups vegetable or chicken stock
2 zucchini, quartered and sliced
4 tsp. capers, rinsed and chopped
Handful of fresh basil leaves, torn
Salt and ground black pepper

Heat the oil in a large saucepan. Add the onion and garlic, and cook gently for 5 minutes. Add the tomatoes, bell pepper, tomato paste, and stock, and bring to a boil. Reduce the heat, cover, and simmer for 10 minutes.

Add the zucchini and capers, and simmer for a further 10 minutes, until tender. Stir in the basil leaves and salt and pepper to taste. Ladle the soup into bowls and serve.

Serves 4

chunky root vegetable soup

see variations page 77

This satisfying soup is packed with vegetables to make a nutritious, filling lunch or dinner.

2 tbsp. olive oil
1 onion, finely chopped
1 garlic clove, crushed
3 carrots, roughly chopped
3 celery sticks, cubed
3 small turnips, peeled and cubed

14-oz. can chopped tomatoes
1 tbsp. tomato paste
5 cups vegetable or chicken stock
1 tsp. fresh oregano leaves
Salt and ground black pepper

Heat the oil in a large saucepan. Add the onion and garlic, and cook gently for 5 minutes. Add the carrots, celery, turnips, tomatoes, tomato paste, stock, and oregano. Stir well and bring to a boil.

Reduce the heat, cover the pan, and simmer the soup for about 20 minutes, until the vegetables are tender. Add salt and pepper to taste before serving the soup.

Serves 4

variations

chicken noodle soup

see base recipe page 49

creamy chicken noodle soup
Prepare the basic recipe and stir in 1/2 cup heavy cream just before serving.

chicken noodle soup with scallions
Prepare the basic recipe, adding 1 bunch sliced scallions about 1 minute before the end of cooking time.

chicken noodle soup with chorizo
Prepare the basic recipe, adding 2 oz. chopped chorizo to the broth with the chicken meat.

hot & spicy chicken noodle soup
Prepare the basic recipe, adding 2 chopped, seeded, red chilies with the other vegetables.

chicken noodle soup with apricots
Prepare the basic recipe, adding 12 chopped ready-to-eat dried apricots to the strained broth. Simmer for 15 minutes before adding the noodles, and continue as in the main recipe.

spiced lentil, chickpea & chorizo soup

see base recipe page 51

vegetarian spiced lentil & chickpea soup
Prepare the basic recipe, using vegetable stock, and omitting the chorizo.

spiced lentil, navy bean & chorizo soup
Prepare the basic recipe, using navy beans in place of the chickpeas.

thick spiced lentil, chickpea & chorizo soup
Prepare the basic recipe. Before seasoning and adding lemon juice, ladle half the soup into a food processor or blender and blend until smooth. Return the smooth soup to the saucepan and heat gently. Season and add lemon juice to taste, then serve.

spiced lentil, chickpea & chorizo soup with spicy harissa
Prepare the basic recipe, adding 1 teaspoon harissa (hot chili paste) to the soup with the other spices.

spiced lentil, chickpea & chorizo soup with fresh cilantro
Prepare the basic recipe. Sprinkle chopped fresh cilantro into the soup just before serving.

variations

carrot, leek & potato soup

see base recipe page 52

carrot, leek & potato soup with mustard
Prepare the basic recipe, stirring 1 tablespoon whole-grain mustard into the soup before adding salt and pepper.

carrot, leek & potato soup with cheese
Prepare the basic recipe, ladle into bowls and serve sprinkled with grated cheddar or monterey jack cheese.

carrot, leek & beet soup
Prepare the basic recipe, using 1 peeled and diced cooked beet in place of the potato.

carrot, leek, potato & tomato soup
Prepare the basic recipe, adding one 14-oz. can chopped tomatoes with the other vegetables.

carrot, leek & potato soup with mustard and cheese
Prepare the basic recipe, adding 1 tablespoon whole-grain mustard when puréeing the soup, and sprinkle with grated cheddar (or other) cheese before serving.

variations

sweet-and-sour red cabbage soup with bacon

see base recipe page 55

vegetarian sweet-and-sour red cabbage soup
Prepare the basic recipe, omitting the bacon.

sweet-and-sour red cabbage & beet soup with bacon
Prepare the basic recipe, adding 1 raw or cooked beet, peeled and cut into matchstick strips, with the cabbage.

fruity sweet-and-sour red cabbage soup with bacon
Prepare the basic recipe, adding a handful of golden raisins with the cabbage.

spiced sweet-and-sour red cabbage soup with bacon
Prepare the basic recipe, adding 1 teaspoon crushed cumin seeds and 1 teaspoon ground coriander with the other spices.

sweet-and-sour red cabbage soup with bacon & chickpeas
Prepare the basic recipe, adding one 14-oz. can drained, rinsed chickpeas to the pan with the cabbage.

variations

ribollita

see base recipe page 56

classic ribollita
Prepare the basic recipe, using shredded Tuscan kale (cavolo nero cabbage) in place of the Savoy cabbage.

mixed bean ribollita
Prepare the basic recipe, using one 14-oz. can mixed beans in place of the cannellini beans.

spicy ribollita
Prepare the basic recipe, adding 1/2 teaspoon crushed dried chili with the tomatoes.

rustic ciabatta ribollita
Prepare the basic recipe. Tear half a ciabatta loaf into chunks and add them to the soup just before ladling it into bowls.

rich vegetable ribollita
Prepare the basic recipe, adding 2 chopped carrots and 4 chopped celery stalks with the tomatoes.

green bean soup with tuna & tapenade toasts

see base recipe page 59

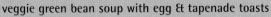

veggie green bean soup with egg & tapenade toasts
Prepare the basic recipe, but omit the anchovies from the tapenade, and omit the tuna. Top each toast with a quarter of a hard-cooked egg.

fava bean soup with tuna & tapenade toasts
Prepare the basic recipe, using shelled fava beans instead of green beans.

mixed bean soup with tuna & tapenade toasts
Prepare the basic recipe, using a mixture of half fava and half green beans instead of all green beans.

simple green bean soup
Prepare the basic recipe, omitting the tapenade and tuna toasts, and serve with chunks of crusty bread.

variations

black bean soup with sour cream

see base recipe page 60

red kidney bean soup with sour cream
Prepare the basic soup, using kidney beans in place of the black beans.

black bean soup with sour cream & parsley
Prepare the basic recipe, garnishing the bowls of soup with chopped fresh parsley in place of the cilantro.

black-eyed pea soup with sour cream
Prepare the basic recipe, using black-eyed peas in place of the black beans.

black bean soup with tomatoes, sour cream & salsa
Prepare the basic recipe, adding a 14-oz. can chopped tomatoes with the stock. Serve topped with sour cream and a spoonful of tomato salsa.

black bean soup with tortilla chips, sour cream & scallions
Prepare the basic recipe. Serve topped with tortilla chips, sour cream, and shredded scallions.

variations

beef & barley soup

see base recipe page 63

lamb & barley soup
Prepare the basic recipe, using cubed lamb in place of the beef.

chicken & barley soup
Prepare the basic recipe, using 3 cubed, skinless, chicken breasts in place of the beef, and chicken stock in place of the beef stock. Add the chicken with the vegetables, rather than with the barley.

beef & barley soup with tomatoes
Prepare the basic recipe, adding one 14-oz. can chopped tomatoes with the barley.

beef & barley soup with oregano
Prepare the basic recipe, using fresh oregano in place of the thyme. Sprinkle with fresh oregano leaves before serving.

variations

mediterranean vegetable soup

see base recipe page 64

mediterranean vegetable soup with pesto
Prepare the basic recipe, and drizzle each serving with a little pesto.

mediterranean vegetable soup with pasta
Prepare the basic recipe, adding a good handful of small pasta shapes, such as rotini, to the pan with the zucchini.

mediterranean vegetable soup with parmesan
Prepare the basic recipe. Serve the soup sprinkled with shavings of Parmesan cheese.

mediterranean vegetable soup with pesto bruschetta
Prepare the basic recipe. Toast 8 slices of baguette until golden on both sides, then spread with pesto and top with a drained charbroiled artichoke in olive oil. Serve the bruschetta with the soup.

mediterranean vegetable soup with green beans
Prepare the basic recipe, adding 1/4 lb. trimmed, sliced green beans with the zucchini.

chunky root vegetable soup

see base recipe page 67

smooth root vegetable soup
Prepare the basic recipe. Blend the soup until smooth in a food processor
or blender before serving. Add a little more stock if the soup is too thick.

chunky root vegetable soup with bacon
Prepare the basic recipe, adding 3 roughly chopped, bacon strips with the
onion and garlic.

chunky beet & mixed vegetable soup
Prepare the basic recipe, using 1 large peeled and diced raw beet in place
of the turnips.

chunky root vegetable soup with black-eyed beans
Prepare the basic recipe, adding one 14-oz. can drained, rinsed black-eyed
peas with the vegetables.

smooth &
creamy

A big pot of rich, creamy soup offers ultimate
comfort in its simplest form. Mild or bold, rich
and flavorsome, or hot and spicy, there's something
for everyone in this chapter.

fennel soup with blue cheese

see variations page 98

With a subtle aniseed flavor, cut by the sharp tang of blue cheese, this smooth creamy soup makes an utterly luxurious feast, served with chunks of crusty bread.

2 tbsp. (1/4 stick) butter
2 onions, chopped
3 bulbs of fennel
1 potato, chopped

4 1/4 cups vegetable stock
Generous 3/4 cup light cream
2–3 oz. blue cheese, crumbled
Salt and ground black pepper

Melt the butter in a large saucepan. Add the onions and cook gently for about 4 minutes. Meanwhile, trim the fennel leaves from the bulbs and reserve them for garnish, then slice the bulbs and add to the pan with the potato and stock. Bring to a boil. Reduce the heat, cover, and simmer for about 20 minutes, until the vegetables are tender.

Process the soup in a food processor or blender until smooth. Return the soup to the pan. Stir in the cream, about three-quarters of the cheese, and salt and pepper to taste.

Warm through, then ladle the soup into bowls. Sprinkle with the remaining cheese and fennel leaves, and serve.

Serves 4

wild mushroom soup with sage

see variations page 99

Make this soup in the fall when wild mushrooms are in season and plentiful.

2 tbsp. (1/4 stick) butter
1 onion, chopped
2 garlic cloves, crushed
1 tbsp. all-purpose flour
4 1/4 cups vegetable or chicken stock
1 1/2 lb. wild mushrooms, chopped

6 fresh sage leaves, chopped
1/2 cup white wine
1/2 cup heavy cream
Salt and ground black pepper
Chopped fresh parsley, to garnish

Melt the butter in a large saucepan. Add the onion and garlic, and cook for about 4 minutes, until softened. Stir in the flour and cook for 1 minute more, then gradually stir in the stock. Add the mushrooms and bring to a boil. Reduce the heat, cover, and simmer gently for about 15 minutes, until the mushrooms are tender. Stir in the sage.

Remove a couple of ladlefuls of the mushrooms and set aside. Process the remaining soup in a food processor or blender until smooth. Return the soup to the pan, add the reserved mushrooms, and stir in the wine, cream, and salt and pepper to taste. Warm through without boiling. Ladle into bowls and sprinkle with parsley to garnish.

Serves 4

almond & garlic soup with fresh grapes

see variations page 100

This classic Spanish soup is very rich and therefore served in small portions — making it the perfect appetizer.

3/4 cup blanched almonds
2 garlic cloves, crushed
1/3 cup fresh white breadcrumbs
2 1/2 cups cold vegetable stock

1 tbsp. sherry vinegar
Ground black pepper
1 1/3 cups green grapes, peeled and halved
Ice cubes, to serve (optional)

Heat a nonstick skillet. Add the almonds and stir over a low heat for about 3 minutes, until toasted. Place in a food processor or blender and process to a fine powder. Add the garlic, breadcrumbs, and about one fourth of the stock, then process to a smooth paste. Gradually add the rest of the stock, blending to a smooth soup.

Pour the soup into a bowl. Stir in the vinegar and pepper to taste. Chill for at least 2 hours. To serve, check the seasoning, adding more pepper if required, then ladle the soup into bowls. Add a few ice cubes to each portion (if using), and sprinkle the grapes over the top.

Serves 4

spinach & coconut soup

see variations page 101

Rich with coconut milk and fragrant with spices, this intriguing soup makes a great alternative to most classic cream soups and is great for those on a dairy-free diet.

2 tbsp. sunflower oil
1 onion, chopped
2 garlic cloves, crushed
2 green chilies, seeded and chopped
2 tsp. ground cumin
1 tsp. ground coriander
1/2 tsp. turmeric

1/2 tsp. ground ginger
2 1/2 cups vegetable stock
2 1/2 cups coconut milk
Generous 1 lb. spinach
Juice of 1/2 lemon, to taste
Salt
Coconut shavings, toasted, to garnish (optional)

Heat the oil in a large saucepan. Add the onion, garlic, and chilies, and cook gently for about 4 minutes. Stir in the cumin, coriander, turmeric, and ginger, then add the stock and coconut milk, and bring to a boil. Reduce the heat, cover the pan, and simmer the soup for about 10 minutes.

Stir in the spinach and cook for about 2 minutes, until the leaves wilt. Process about three-fourths of the soup in a food processor or blender until smooth. Return the smooth soup to the pan, stir in lemon juice, and salt to taste. Heat gently for a few seconds, if necessary, then ladle into serving bowls. Sprinkle with coconut shavings, if desired, and serve.

Serves 4

roasted bell pepper & mascarpone soup

see variations page 102

Sweet, smooth, and creamy, with a deliciously rich, and slight smoky flavor, this soup is excellent in summer and early fall when bell peppers and tomatoes are at their best.

6 red bell peppers
2 tbsp. olive oil
1 onion, chopped
2 garlic cloves, crushed
3 ripe tomatoes, peeled and chopped

5 cups vegetable stock
6 tbsp. mascarpone cheese
Handful of fresh basil leaves, plus extra
    to garnish
Salt and ground black pepper

Preheat the oven to 450°F (230°C). Arrange the peppers on a cookie sheet and cook for about 30 minutes, until charred. Transfer the peppers to a bowl, cover with plastic wrap, and let stand for 15 minutes, until cool enough to handle.

Heat the oil in a large saucepan, then cook the onion and garlic for 4 minutes. Add the tomatoes and stock. Boil, reduce the heat, cover, and simmer for 10 minutes.

Peel the peppers, remove the seeds, and put the flesh in a food processor or blender with any juices. Add the mascarpone. Pour in the soup, add the basil, and process until smooth. Season with salt and pepper to taste, and serve sprinkled with fresh basil leaves.

Serves 4

creamy zucchini & dill soup

see variations page 103

Smooth, mild, creamy, and gently flavored with aromatic dill, this soup tastes wonderfully luxurious without being too rich.

2 tbsp. olive oil
1 onion, chopped
2 garlic cloves, crushed
8 zucchini, sliced
4 1/4 cups vegetable or chicken stock

1 1/2 tbsp. dried or fresh dill, plus extra fresh dill to garnish
1/2 cup light cream
Salt and ground black pepper
Juice of about 1/4 lemon, to taste

Heat the oil in a large saucepan. Add the onion and garlic, and cook for about 5 minutes. Stir in the zucchini and stock, and bring to a boil. Reduce the heat, cover, and simmer gently for 5 to 10 minutes, until the zucchini are tender.

Add the dill, then process the soup in a food processor or blender until smooth. Add the cream, and salt and pepper to taste, and pulse to mix. Squeeze in a little lemon juice to taste, then ladle the soup into bowls and serve garnished with dill.

Serves 4

cream of wine & mussel soup

see variations page 104

This sophisticated soup is perfect as an appetizer and just as good for a light meal, served with chunks of crusty white bread.

3 lb. 5 oz. mussels, cleaned
3 tbsp. butter
3 garlic cloves, crushed
1 1/4 cups white wine

3 1/4 cups fish stock
2/3 cup heavy cream
2 tbsp. chopped fresh parsley
Salt and ground black pepper

Discard any open mussels that do not close when tapped sharply. Heat the butter in a large saucepan and fry the garlic for 1 minute. Add the mussels, pour in half the wine, cover the pan tightly, and cook over high heat to steam the mussels until their shells are open, about 4 minutes.

Drain the mussels through a colander or fine sieve placed over a clean saucepan. Stand the colander over a bowl and put aside. Add the remaining wine and stock to the strained liquor, and heat gently until simmering.

Discard any shells that have not opened. Shell about two-thirds of the mussels and add them to the soup. Warm through for a few seconds, then remove the pan from the heat.

Stir in the cream, parsley, and salt and pepper to taste. Ladle the soup into bowls and garnish with the remaining mussels in their shells.

Serves 4

cream of onion soup with chives

see variations page 105

This thick and rich soup is perfect on a cold, dark evening, when you need a little warming, comfort food.

2 tbsp. olive oil
3 Spanish onions, chopped
1 small potato, diced
5 cups vegetable or chicken stock
3/4 cup light cream

2 tbsp. snipped fresh chives, plus extra
    to garnish
Salt and ground black pepper
Breadsticks, to serve

Heat the oil in a large saucepan. Add the onions and cook gently for about 20 minutes, until soft and translucent. Add the potato and stir in the stock. Bring the soup to a boil. Reduce the heat, cover, and simmer for about 10 minutes, until the potato is tender.

Process the soup in a food processor or blender until smooth. Return the soup to the rinsed-out pan. Stir in the cream, chives, and salt and pepper to taste. Reheat without boiling.

Ladle the soup into serving bowls and sprinkle with more chives. Serve immediately, while piping hot, with breadsticks.

Serves 4

watercress soup

see variations page 106

This light, cream soup is the perfect way to cook peppery watercress. Serve it as an appetizer, or a light meal with big chunks of crusty bread.

2 tbsp. (1/4 stick) butter
1 onion, chopped
1 potato, chopped
3 1/4 cups vegetable or chicken stock

8 oz. watercress
1 1/4 cups milk
1/4 cup heavy cream
Salt and ground black pepper

Melt the butter in a large saucepan. Add the onion and cook gently for 4 minutes. Add the potato, stir in the stock, and bring to a boil. Reduce the heat, cover, and simmer gently for about 15 minutes, or until the potato is tender.

Meanwhile, gently pull the leaves off the watercress and shred the stalks. Add the stalks to the soup and simmer for about 1 minute, then add three-fourths of the leaves, and simmer for 1 minute more.

Process the soup in a food processor or blender until smooth. Return the soup to the rinsed-out pan, stir in the milk and cream, and warm through without boiling. Reserve a few of the remaining watercress leaves for garnish, then stir the rest into the soup, with salt and pepper to taste. Serve sprinkled with the last of the watercress.

Serves 4

potato & garlic soup

see variations page 107

Velvety smooth and full of fragrant garlic, this simple soup is robust and comforting.

2 tbsp. olive oil
1 onion, chopped
6 garlic cloves, crushed
2 large potatoes, chopped
3 1/2 cups chicken stock

1 3/4 cups milk
Juice of about 1/2 lemon, to taste
Salt and ground black pepper
1/4 cup light cream
2 tbsp. chopped fresh parsley

Heat the oil in a large saucepan. Add the onion and garlic, and cook gently for about 4 minutes. Stir in the potatoes and stock, and bring to a boil. Reduce the heat, cover, and simmer for about 15 minutes, until the potatoes are tender.

Process the soup in a food processor or blender until smooth. Return the soup to the rinsed-out pan, add the milk, and heat through without boiling. Stir in lemon juice, and salt and pepper to taste.

To serve, ladle the soup into bowls, drizzle a tablespoon of cream into each bowl, add a grinding of black pepper, and sprinkle with parsley.

Serves 4

variations

fennel soup with blue cheese

see base recipe page 79

celery root soup with blue cheese & chives
Prepare the basic recipe, using 1 lb. celery root in place of the fennel and potato, and sprinkle with chives to garnish.

fennel soup with goat cheese
Prepare the basic recipe, using 3–4 oz. cubed goat cheese in place of the blue cheese

fennel soup with blue cheese & pear croûtes
Prepare the basic recipe. Toast 4 slices of baguette until golden on both sides. Top each with an extra slice of blue cheese, and a wedge of ripe pear. Float on top of the soup and serve.

fennel soup with goat cheese toasts
Prepare the basic recipe, omitting the blue cheese. Toast 4 slices of walnut bread on one side. Turn over, spread with goat cheese, and place under a hot broiler until the cheese begins to melt, then serve with the soup.

fennel & celery soup with blue cheese
Prepare the basic recipe, using 2 fennel bulbs and 6 sliced celery stalks.

wild mushroom soup with sage

see base recipe page 81

wild mushroom soup with thyme
Prepare the basic recipe, adding 1 teaspoon fresh thyme leaves with the stock, and omitting the sage.

cheater's wild mushroom soup with sage
Prepare the basic recipe, using cultivated mushrooms instead of wild fungi. Soak 1/2 oz. dried porcini in a little boiling water for 20 minutes, then add to the soup, including the soaking water, with the stock.

wild mushroom soup with garlic toasts
Prepare the basic recipe. Beat 1/4 cup (1/2 stick) soft butter with 2 crushed garlic cloves, and season with black pepper. Toast 8 slices of baguette, spread with the garlic butter, and serve with the soup.

wild mushroom & chicken soup with sage
Prepare the basic recipe. Shred 2 skinless, cooked chicken breasts, stir into the soup, and warm through before serving.

wild mushroom soup with sage & crispy bacon
Prepare the basic recipe. To serve, broil 3 slices bacon until crisp, then snip them into bite-size pieces, and sprinkle over the soup.

almond & garlic soup with fresh grapes

see base recipe page 82

hazelnut & garlic soup with fresh grapes
Prepare the basic soup, using blanched hazelnuts in place of the almonds.

almond & garlic soup with garlic toasts
Prepare the basic recipe. To serve, toast 8 slices baguette on both sides until golden. Rub one side of each with a cut garlic clove, and drizzle with extra virgin olive oil. Serve with the soup instead of the grapes.

almond & garlic soup with grapes & fresh mint
Prepare the basic recipe, sprinkling each serving with chopped fresh mint.

almond & garlic soup with grapes & fresh parsley
Prepare the basic recipe, sprinkling each serving with chopped fresh parsley.

almond & garlic soup with grapes & scallions
Prepare the basic recipe. Thinly slice 2 scallions and sprinkle over the soup with the grapes.

variations

spinach & coconut soup

see base recipe page 85

curried spinach & coconut soup
Prepare the basic recipe, using 2 tablespoons curry paste in place of
the cumin, coriander, turmeric, and ginger.

thai-style spinach & coconut soup
Prepare the basic recipe, using 2 tablespoons green curry paste in place
of the cumin, coriander, and turmeric.

broccoli & coconut soup
Prepare the basic recipe, using broccoli in place of the spinach. Cut
the broccoli into florets, and cook for about 10 minutes, until tender,
before blending.

cream of spinach soup
Prepare the basic recipe, using 4 1/4 cups vegetable stock, and omitting the
chili, cumin, coriander, turmeric, ginger, and coconut milk. Stir in 1/2 cup
light cream just before serving, and season with salt, pepper, and freshly
grated nutmeg to taste.

variations

roasted bell pepper & mascarpone soup

see base recipe page 86

chilled roasted bell pepper & mascarpone soup
Prepare the basic recipe and let the soup cool. Chill for at least 2 hours and serve sprinkled with fresh basil leaves.

roasted bell pepper & crème fraîche soup
Prepare the basic recipe, using crème fraîche in place of mascarpone. Serve topped with a dollop of crème fraîche and fresh basil leaves.

roasted bell pepper & mascarpone soup with chives
Prepare the basic recipe, omitting the basil. Stir 2 tablespoons snipped chives into the blended soup, and serve sprinkled with more chives.

roasted mixed bell pepper & mascarpone soup
Prepare the basic recipe, using a mixture of red, orange, and yellow bell peppers.

spicy roasted bell pepper & mascarpone soup
Prepare the basic recipe, adding 2 seeded, chopped red chilies with the onion and garlic.

variations

creamy zucchini & dill soup

see base recipe page 89

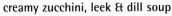

creamy zucchini, leek & dill soup
Prepare the basic recipe, using 1 large sliced leek in place of the onion.

creamy zucchini & chive soup
Prepare the basic recipe, omitting the dill. Stir 2 tablespoons snipped chives into the blended soup, and serve sprinkled with more snipped chives.

creamy zucchini, spinach & dill soup
Prepare the basic recipe, adding 3 large handfuls of spinach about 2 minutes before the end of cooking time. Blend and season as before.

creamy zucchini, broccoli & dill soup
Prepare the basic recipe, using 3 zucchini and adding 1 large head of broccoli, cut into bite-size florets.

chilled creamy zucchini & dill soup
Prepare the basic recipe, then let the soup cool, and chill for at least 2 hours before serving.

variations

cream of wine & mussel soup

see base recipe page 90

creamy mussel soup with vermouth
Prepare the basic recipe, using vermouth in place of the white wine.

cream of wine & mussel soup with chives
Prepare the basic recipe, using snipped chives in place of the parsley.

cream of hard cider & mussel soup
Prepare the basic recipe, using hard cider in place of the white wine.

cream of wine & mussel soup with shallots
Prepare the basic recipe, using 3 finely chopped shallots and reducing the garlic to 1 crushed clove.

creamy wine & crab soup
Prepare the basic recipe, omitting the mussels. Stir in two 6-oz. cans white crabmeat with the stock.

variations

cream of onion soup with chives

see base recipe page 93

cream of onion soup with white wine & chives
Prepare the basic recipe, using 4 1/4 cups stock and 3/4 cup white wine.

cream of onion soup with thyme
Prepare the basic recipe, adding 1 teaspoon fresh thyme leaves with the stock, and omitting the chives.

cream of onion soup with chives & garlic croûtes
Prepare the basic recipe. To serve, slice a small baguette diagonally. Toast the slices on both sides until golden, then spread with garlic butter, and serve with the soup.

cream of onion soup with scallions
Prepare the basic recipe, sprinkling the soup with sliced scallions instead of chives.

variations

watercress soup

see base recipe page 94

chilled watercress soup
Prepare the basic recipe, then leave to cool, and chill for at least 2 hours before serving.

watercress & scallion soup
Prepare the basic recipe, adding 1 bunch sliced scallions with the watercress.

dairy-free watercress soup
Prepare the basic recipe, using soy milk in place of dairy milk. (Be careful not to boil the soup or it will curdle.)

watercress & spinach soup
Prepare the basic recipe, adding 2 handfuls of spinach with the watercress.

potato & garlic soup

see base recipe page 97

potato & garlic soup with sage
Prepare the basic recipe, using 2 teaspoons chopped fresh sage in place of the parsley.

potato, leek & garlic soup
Prepare the basic recipe, using 1 sliced leek in place of the onion.

potato, carrot & garlic soup
Prepare the basic recipe, using 1 potato and 3 sliced carrots.

potato & garlic soup with potato chips
Prepare the basic recipe. Serve the soup topped with a handful of lightly crushed potato chips.

potato & garlic soup with crispy bacon
Prepare the basic recipe. To serve, broil 4 bacon slices until crisp, then snip them into pieces over the bowls of soup.

meal in a bowl

Hearty and nutritious, wholesome and full-flavored

soups make fabulous feasts in a single bowl.

Whichever delicious recipe you choose from

this chapter, it's sure to keep you satisfied until

your next meal.

chunky seafood soup

see variations page 128

There are countless stewlike fish soups, such as French bouillabaise, that make the most of the catch of the day. This chunky broth takes its inspiration from those classic origins.

2 tbsp. olive oil
1 onion, finely chopped
3 garlic cloves, crushed
14-oz. can chopped tomatoes
3 1/2 cups fish stock
1/4 tsp. crushed dried chili
1 tsp. fresh thyme leaves

1 1/2 lb. mussels, cleaned
1 lb. firm white fish, cut into
    bite-size chunks
1/2 lb. raw shrimp, shelled and deveined
Salt and ground black pepper
2 tbsp. chopped fresh parsley
Crusty bread, to serve

Heat the oil in a large saucepan. Add the onion and garlic, and cook for 4 minutes. Add the tomatoes, stock, chili, and thyme. Boil, reduce the heat, cover, and simmer for 20 minutes.

Discard any open mussels that do not close when tapped sharply. Bring 1/4 cup water to the boil in a large saucepan. Add the mussels, cover tightly, and cook for about 5 minutes, until the shells open. Drain the mussels, discarding any unopened shells. Shell about three-fourths of the mussels, then set all of them aside.

Add the fish and shrimp to the soup, and simmer for 2 to 3 minutes, until the fish is cooked through, and the shrimp are pink. Add all the mussels and heat through for a few seconds. Add salt and pepper to taste, sprinkle with the parsley, and serve with chunks of bread.

Serves 4

chili beef soup with cheese-topped tortilla chips

see variations page 129

This hearty soup makes a warming meal for the whole family. Serve with more tortilla chips or chunks of crusty bread on the side.

2 tbsp. olive oil
1 onion, finely chopped
2 garlic cloves, crushed
3 red chilies, seeded and chopped
8 oz. ground beef
2 tsp. ground cumin
14-oz. can chopped tomatoes
1 tsp. sun-dried tomato paste

3 1/2 cups beef stock
1/2 tsp. fresh thyme leaves
1 green bell pepper, seeded and chopped
14-oz. can kidney beans, rinsed and drained
Salt and ground black pepper
2 handfuls tortilla chips
Cheddar cheese, grated, for sprinkling

Heat the oil in a large saucepan. Add the onion, garlic, and chilies, and cook gently for about 4 minutes. Add the beef and fry for about 5 minutes, stirring often, until browned all over. Stir in the cumin, tomatoes, sun-dried tomato paste, stock, and thyme, and bring to a boil. Reduce the heat, cover, and simmer for about 15 minutes.

Add the pepper and beans to the soup, and simmer for a further 10 minutes. Stir in salt and pepper to taste. Ladle the soup into bowls and top each portion with tortilla chips and a sprinkling of cheese. Serve immediately.

Serves 4

moroccan-style lamb soup with couscous

see variations page 130

This meaty soup is a contemporary take on the traditional Morrocan tagine, cooked with lamb, spices, and dried apricots.

3 tbsp. olive oil
1 onion, finely chopped
2 garlic cloves, crushed
12 oz. lean lamb, cubed
1/4 tsp. cayenne pepper
1 tsp. paprika
1 tsp. ground cumin
1 tsp. ground coriander

2 tsp. ground cinnamon
14-oz. can chopped tomatoes
6 1/4 cups lamb or beef stock
2/3 cup ready-to-eat dried apricots, halved
3/4 cup couscous
3/4 cup boiling water
Salt and ground black pepper
2 tbsp. chopped fresh mint

Heat 2 tablespoons of the oil in a large saucepan. Add the onion and garlic and cook gently for 4 minutes. Stir in the lamb, cayenne, paprika, cumin, coriander, cinnamon, tomatoes, stock, and apricots. Boil, reduce the heat, cover, and simmer for 1 1/2 hours, until the lamb is tender. Put the couscous in a medium bowl, season with salt, and use a fork to mix in the remaining oil. Pour in the water and leave to soak for 5 minutes. Fluff up the couscous, stir in most of the mint, and divide among four bowls, mounding the couscous in the center of each bowl. Add salt and pepper to the soup, then ladle it around the couscous. Sprinkle with the remaining mint.

Serves 4

smoked haddock & sugar snap pea chowder

see variations page 131

Salty smoked haddock and tender sugar snap peas make a great combination in this hearty, chunky fish broth.

2 tbsp. olive oil
1 onion, finely chopped
2 cups fish stock
12 oz. smoked haddock
2 large potatoes, diced

3 cups milk
8 oz. (approx.) sugar snap peas, sliced open
2 tbsp. chopped fresh parsley
Salt and ground black pepper

Heat the oil in a large saucepan. Add the onion and cook gently for 5 minutes. Pour in the stock, add the haddock, and heat until barely simmering. Poach for about 6 minutes, until the fish is cooked. Use a spatula to remove the fish. Add the potatoes to the pan and bring to a boil. Reduce the heat, cover, and simmer for 10 minutes, until the potatoes are tender.

Skin the haddock and break the flesh into large flakes, discarding any bones. Ladle half the soup into a food processor or blender and process until smooth, then return it to the pan. Add the milk and sugar snap peas, and heat gently until almost simmering. Replace the fish and reheat for about 2 minutes, until the sugar snaps are just tender. Add the parsley, salt and pepper to taste, and serve.

Serves 4

pasta & meatball soup

see variations page 132

This chunky, hearty soup is great when you want a comforting and substantial meal.

8 oz. lean ground beef
1/2 onion, grated
2 garlic cloves, crushed
1/2 tsp. dried oregano
1 tbsp. grated Parmesan cheese, plus shavings
   to garnish
Salt and ground black pepper

1 tbsp. olive oil
14-oz. can chopped tomatoes
3 1/4 cups beef stock
1 tbsp. tomato paste
3–4 oz. conchigliette or other small
   pasta shapes
Fresh oregano leaves, to garnish

To make the meatballs, mix the beef, onion, half the garlic, half the oregano, and the Parmesan, and season well with salt and pepper. Roll the mixture into about 20 bite-size meatballs.

Heat the oil in a large saucepan. Working in batches if necessary, add the meatballs and brown them all over. Transfer the meatballs to a plate when browned.

Add the remaining garlic to the pan and cook for 1 minute. Add the browned meatballs, tomatoes, stock, tomato paste, and remaining oregano. Add salt and pepper to taste and simmer gently for about 15 minutes.

Add the pasta and simmer for a further 8 to 10 minutes, until tender. Taste the soup and add more salt and pepper, if necessary, then serve sprinkled with Parmesan and oregano.

Serves 4

spicy sausage & bean soup

see variations page 133

This soup makes a hearty treat and is particularly good after a cold winter walk. It can be made ahead and reheated before serving.

2 tbsp. olive oil
5 good-quality pork sausages
1 onion, chopped
2 garlic cloves, finely chopped
1 1/2 red chilies, seeded and chopped
14-oz. can chopped tomatoes

3 1/4 cups beef or chicken stock
Two 14-oz. cans cranberry beans or cannellini
    beans, drained and rinsed
2 tbsp. chopped fresh parsley
Salt and ground black pepper

Heat the oil in a large saucepan. Add the sausages, brown them all over, and then remove. Add the onion, garlic, and chilies to the pan, and fry gently for 3 minutes.

Cut the sausages into thick slices and return them to the pan, adding the tomatoes and stock. Bring to a boil, then reduce the heat, cover, and simmer gently for 20 minutes.

Put half the beans in a food processor or blender and add a couple of ladlefuls of the soup stock. Process until smooth, then stir the purée into the soup with the remaining beans, and simmer for a further 10 minutes. Add salt and pepper to taste, and stir in the parsley before serving the soup.

Serves 4

roasted squash risotto soup with goat cheese

see variations page 134

This wholesome soup — a liquid risotto — makes a wonderfully sustaining meal.

1 butternut squash, seeded, peeled, and cut
   into chunks
3 tbsp. olive oil
Salt and ground black pepper
1 onion, finely chopped
2 garlic cloves, chopped
1 cup risotto rice

3/4 cup white wine
5 cups vegetable or chicken stock
6 fresh sage leaves, chopped, plus extra
   to garnish
4 oz. goat cheese, cut into
   bite-size pieces

Preheat the oven to 400°F (200°C). Put the squash in a large baking dish, drizzle 1 tablespoon of the oil over all, and add salt and pepper to taste. Toss to coat the squash thoroughly and roast for about 30 minutes, until tender.

Meanwhile, heat the remaining oil in a large saucepan. Add the onion and garlic, and cook gently for 5 minutes. Add the rice and cook for 2 minutes, stirring, then pour in the wine and simmer gently, stirring, until most of the wine has been absorbed. Stir in the stock and bring to a boil. Reduce the heat and simmer gently, stirring frequently, for about 20 minutes, until the rice is tender. Stir the sage and roasted squash into the soup, add salt and pepper to taste. Ladle the soup into bowls, sprinkle with goat cheese, and garnish with sage.

Serves 4

vermicelli soup with clams

see variations page 135

This fragrant, zesty broth is packed with tender clams and filling pasta to make a fabulous meal. Serve chunks of crusty baguette to mop up the broth.

2 lb. clams, cleaned
2 tbsp. olive oil
1 onion, finely chopped
2 garlic cloves, crushed
1/2 cup vermouth
14-oz. can chopped tomatoes

5 cups fish stock
1 tsp. finely grated orange zest
Juice of 2 oranges
8 oz. vermicelli
2 tbsp. chopped fresh parsley
Salt and ground black pepper

Discard any open clams that do not close when tapped sharply. Heat the oil in a large saucepan. Add the onion and garlic, and cook gently for 5 minutes. Add the clams and vermouth, cover, and cook over fairly high heat for about 4 minutes, until the clams have opened. Remove the clams using a slotted spoon and set aside. Add the tomatoes, stock, orange zest, and juice. Bring to the boil. Reduce the heat, cover, and simmer for 10 minutes.

Meanwhile, discard any clams that have not opened. Reserve about 12 clams in their shells and shell the rest of the clams.

Add the vermicelli to the soup and cook for about 2 minutes, until tender. Add the shelled clams and warm through. Add the parsley and salt and pepper to taste. Serve the soup garnished with the reserved clams in their shells.

Serves 4

spicy chicken & sweet potato soup with coconut milk

see variations page 136

Spicy, creamy, and fragrant with peppery ginger, this delicious soup is packed with chunks of chicken and sweet potato to make a real meal in a bowl.

2 tbsp. sunflower oil
1 onion, finely chopped
3 garlic cloves, crushed
2 tsp. grated fresh ginger
2 green chilies, seeded and finely chopped
1/2 tsp. ground turmeric
2 tsp. ground cumin
1 tsp. ground coriander

2 sweet potatoes, diced
2 skinless, boneless, chicken breasts, cut into
    bite-size pieces
14-oz. can coconut milk
3 1/2 cups chicken stock
Juice of about 1/2 lemon, to taste
Salt and ground black pepper
Chopped fresh cilantro, to serve

Heat the oil in a large saucepan. Add the onion and cook gently for 3 minutes. Add the garlic, ginger, and chilies, and fry for a further 2 minutes. Stir in the turmeric, cumin, and coriander. Add the sweet potatoes, chicken, coconut milk, and stock. Bring to a boil. Reduce the heat, cover, and simmer for 15 minutes, until the chicken and potatoes are cooked.

Crush about half the sweet potato using the back of a spoon or fork, and stir to mix. Add lemon juice and salt and pepper to taste, then sprinkle with cilantro, and serve.

Serves 4

pork & chickpea soup with zesty orange

see variations page 137

Lightly spiced and fragrant with orange, this cross between broth and stew is perfect when you need something both filling and fabulous.

2 tbsp. olive oil
1 onion, finely chopped
2 garlic cloves, crushed
8 oz. lean pork loin, trimmed, and
    cut into bite-size pieces
2 tsp. ground cumin
2 tsp. ground coriander

Grated zest and juice of 1 orange
14-oz. can chopped tomatoes
3 1/2 cups pork or chicken stock
Salt and ground black pepper
14-oz. can chickpeas, drained and rinsed
2 tbsp. chopped fresh parsley
Juice of about 1/2 lemon, to taste

Heat the oil in a large saucepan. Add the onion and garlic, and cook gently for 4 minutes. Add the pork, sprinkle the cumin and coriander over all, and cook, stirring, for about 1 minute. Stir in the orange zest and juice, tomatoes, stock, and salt and pepper. Bring to a boil, then reduce the heat. Cover the pan and simmer for about 20 minutes.

Stir in the chickpeas and simmer for a further 10 minutes, until the pork is tender. Add more salt and pepper, if necessary, then stir in the parsley and lemon juice to taste before serving.

Serves 4

variations

chunky seafood soup

see base recipe page 109

chunky fish & shrimp soup
Prepare the basic recipe, using 2 lb. firm white fish and 12 oz. shrimp, and omitting the mussels.

chunky seafood soup with fresh cilantro
Prepare the basic recipe, omitting the thyme. Just before serving, stir in a big handful of chopped fresh cilantro.

curried chunky seafood soup
Prepare the basic recipe, adding 2 tablespoons curry paste in place of the thyme. Serve sprinkled with chopped fresh mint.

chunky seafood soup with fresh mint
Prepare the basic recipe, omitting the thyme. Just before serving, stir in 2 teaspoons chopped fresh mint and serve sprinkled with more fresh mint.

smoky seafood soup
Prepare the basic recipe, using smoked haddock in place of the white fish.

chili beef soup with cheese-topped tortilla chips

see base recipe page 111

chili lamb soup with cheese-topped tortilla chips
Prepare the basic recipe, using ground lamb in place of the beef.

chili turkey soup with cheese-topped tortilla chips
Prepare the basic recipe, using ground turkey in place of the beef and
chicken stock in place of the beef stock.

chili pork soup with cheese-topped tortilla chips
Prepare the basic recipe, using ground pork in place of the beef.

rich tomato & beef soup
Prepare the basic recipe, omitting the chili. Add 1 tablespoon (instead of
1 teaspoon) sun-dried tomato paste and 6 shredded sun-dried tomatoes
with the stock. Serve with or without the tortilla chips.

chili beef soup with pasta
Prepare the basic recipe, adding 4 oz. small pasta shapes 5 minutes
before the end of cooking. Simmer until tender, then serve, omitting the
tortilla chips.

variations

moroccan-style lamb soup with couscous

see base recipe page 112

moroccan-style lamb & pepper soup with couscous
Prepare the basic recipe, adding 2 seeded, chopped red bell peppers with the lamb.

moroccan-style chicken soup with couscous
Prepare the basic recipe, using 4 skinless, boneless chicken breasts, cut into bite-size pieces, in place of lamb, and chicken stock in place of the lamb stock. Cook for 30 minutes.

moroccan-style chickpea soup with couscous
Prepare the basic recipe, using two 14-oz. cans drained, rinsed chickpeas in place of the lamb, and vegetable stock in place of the meat stock. Cook the soup for 30 minutes instead of 1 1/2 hours.

moroccan-style fish soup with couscous
Prepare the basic recipe, omitting the lamb and using fish stock. Cook the soup for 30 minutes, then add 1 lb. firm white fish, cut into bite-size pieces, and cook for a further 5 minutes, or until the fish is cooked.

moroccan-style lamb soup with prunes & couscous
Prepare the basic recipe, using ready-to-eat dried prunes in place of apricots.

smoked haddock & sugar snap pea chowder

see base recipe page 115

smoked haddock & sugar snap pea chowder with bacon
Prepare the basic recipe, adding 3 roughly chopped, bacon slices with the onions.

smoked haddock & sugar snap pea chowder with rice
Prepare the basic recipe. Meanwhile, cook 1 cup long-grain rice in a separate pan of boiling water and then drain well. Spoon the rice into bowls and ladle the chowder over the top.

Spiced smoked haddock & sugar snap pea chowder
Prepare the basic recipe, cooking 1 seeded, chopped red chili with the onion.

smoked haddock, sugar snap pea & green bell pepper chowder
Prepare the basic recipe, adding 1 seeded, diced green bell pepper with the potatoes.

smoked haddock & pea chowder
Prepare the basic recipe, adding a generous cup of thawed frozen peas with the milk and omitting the sugar snap peas.

pasta & meatball soup

see base recipe page 116

pasta & turkey meatball soup

Prepare the basic recipe, using ground turkey in place of the beef, and chicken stock in place of the beef stock.

pasta & meatball soup with beans

Prepare the basic recipe, adding a drained, rinsed 14-oz. can navy beans with the pasta.

pasta & pork meatball soup

Prepare the basic recipe, using ground pork in place of the ground beef.

veggie pasta & bean soup

Prepare the basic recipe, omitting the meat and grated Parmesan cheese. Use vegetable stock instead of beef stock. Fry the onion and garlic in the oil for 5 minutes, then add the oregano, tomatoes, and other ingredients. Add two drained, rinsed 14-oz. cans mixed beans in place of meatballs.

variations

spicy sausage & bean soup

see base recipe page 119

veggie sausage soup
Prepare the basic recipe, using vegetarian sausages and vegetable stock.

spicy sausage & bean broth
Prepare the basic recipe, adding one 14-oz. can beans and simmering
without puréeing any of the soup.

not-so-spicy sausage soup
Prepare the basic recipe, omitting the chilies and adding 1 teaspoon paprika.

spicy sausage, bean & roasted red bell pepper soup
Prepare the basic recipe, adding 3 sliced, bottled roasted bell peppers with
the whole beans.

variations

roasted squash risotto soup with goat cheese

see base recipe page 120

roasted squash risotto soup with blue cheese
Prepare the basic recipe, using blue cheese in place of the goat cheese.

roasted squash risotto soup with capers & chives
Prepare the basic recipe, omitting the sage. Stir 2 tablespoons snipped fresh chives and 2 teaspoons chopped capers into the finished soup.

roasted beet risotto soup with goat cheese
Prepare the basic recipe, using 2 to 3 large raw beets in place of the butternut squash. Roast the beets for 40 to 45 minutes.

roasted squash risotto soup with thyme & goat cheese
Prepare the basic recipe, using 1 teaspoon thyme leaves in place of sage.

variations

vermicelli soup with clams

see base recipe page 123

vermicelli soup with mussels
Prepare the basic recipe, using mussels in place of the clams.

vermicelli soup with fish
Prepare the basic recipe, using 12 oz. firm white fish in place of the clams.
Poach the fish until just cooked in the vermouth, then flake into large
chunks, discarding skin and bones, and add to the soup at the last minute
to warm through.

vermicelli soup with chicken
Prepare the basic recipe, using 12 oz. cooked chicken in place of the clams.
Cut the chicken into bite-size chunks and add to the soup at the last minute
to warm through.

vermicelli soup with shrimp
Prepare the basic recipe, omitting the clams. Add 12 oz. peeled, deveined
raw shrimp with the vermicelli, and cook until the shrimp are pink, and the
pasta tender.

variations

spicy chicken & sweet potato soup with coconut milk

see base recipe page 124

spicy chicken & potato soup with coconut milk
Prepare the basic recipe, using ordinary potatoes in place of sweet potatoes.

spicy chicken, sweet potato & spinach soup with coconut milk
Prepare the basic recipe, adding 2 large handfuls of baby spinach (or shredded large leaves) about 2 minutes before the end of cooking time.

spicy chicken & pumpkin soup with coconut milk
Prepare the basic recipe, using pumpkin or 1/2 small butternut squash in place of the sweet potato.

spicy shrimp & sweet potato soup with coconut milk
Prepare the basic recipe, omitting the chicken. About 2 minutes before the end of the cooking time, add 12 oz. shelled and deveined raw tiger shrimp, and simmer until pink and cooked through.

spicy pork & sweet potato soup with coconut milk
Prepare the basic recipe, using 12 oz. diced lean pork loin in place of the chicken.

pork & chickpea soup with zesty orange

see base recipe page 127

chickpea & orange soup

Prepare the basic recipe, omitting the pork, and using vegetable stock. Simmer for 20 minutes, then stir in two 14-oz. cans drained, rinsed, chickpeas and cook for 10 minutes more.

chicken & chickpea soup with zesty orange

Prepare the basic recipe, using 2 skinless, boneless, chicken breasts, cut into bite-size pieces, in place of the pork. Use chicken stock.

lamb & chickpea soup with zesty orange

Prepare the basic recipe, using lean shoulder of lamb, cut into bite-size pieces, in place of the pork. Use lamb or beef stock.

pork & cannellini bean soup with zesty orange

Prepare the basic recipe, using cannellini beans in place of the chickpeas.

20-minute treats

The inspired selections in this chapter can be

cooked in barely longer than the time it takes to

reheat a store-bought can of soup. Even when

you're in a hurry, there's time to stir up a pot of

delicious homemade soup using these practical

recipes, each taking 20 minutes or fewer to prepare.

broccoli soup with parmesan toasts

see variations page 158

To make Parmesan shavings, pare off wafer-thin slices using a vegetable peeler.

2 tbsp. olive oil
1 onion, finely chopped
2 tbsp. all-purpose flour
3 1/4 cups vegetable or chicken stock
1 lb. broccoli, cut into small florets
1 1/2 cups milk
1/2 tsp. freshly grated nutmeg
Salt and ground black pepper

for the toasts

2 tbsp. (1/4 stick) butter, at room temperature
2/3 cup freshly grated Parmesan cheese
8 slices baguette
1 oz. Parmesan cheese, cut into shavings,
    for topping

Heat the oil in a large saucepan. Add the onion and cook gently for about 4 minutes. Stir in the flour and cook for 1 minute, then gradually stir in the stock. Add the broccoli, bring to a boil, then reduce the heat and simmer for about 7 minutes, until the broccoli is tender.

Process the soup in a blender or food processor until smooth, then return it to the pan. Stir in the milk, nutmeg, and salt and pepper to taste, and heat through. Meanwhile, make the toasts. Beat the butter with the grated Parmesan. Toast the slices of baguette on one side under the broiler, then turn and spread with the butter. Top with Parmesan shavings, broil until golden and bubbling, and serve with the soup.

Serves 4

spiced chickpea & lemon soup

see variations page 159

This warming, fragrant soup is delicious at any time of year. Use a can of chopped tomatoes when fresh tomatoes are out of season.

2 tbsp. olive oil
1 onion, chopped
2 garlic cloves, crushed
2 tsp. ground cumin
1 tsp. ground cinnamon
1/4 tsp. ground ginger

Two 14-oz. cans chickpeas
1 lb. ripe tomatoes, peeled and chopped
4 1/4 cups chicken or vegetable stock
2 tbsp. chopped fresh parsley
Salt and ground black pepper
Juice of about 1/2 lemon, to taste

Heat the oil in a large saucepan. Add the onion and garlic, and cook gently for 4 minutes. Stir in the cumin, cinnamon, and ginger, then add half the chickpeas, tomatoes, and most of the stock, reserving about 3/4 cup. Bring to a boil, reduce the heat, and simmer for about 5 minutes.

Meanwhile, process the remaining chickpeas and reserved stock to a smooth purée in a food processor or blender. Stir the purée into the soup. Stir in the parsley. Add salt and pepper, and lemon juice to taste, and serve.

Serves 4

crab & corn chowder

see variations page 160

This rich, spicy chowder may be incredibly simple and quick to make, but it tastes like a sophisticated treat.

2 tbsp. sunflower oil
1 onion, finely chopped
1 garlic clove, crushed
1 red chili, seeded and chopped
2 potatoes, diced
1 red bell pepper, seeded and finely diced

2 1/2 cups fish, vegetable, or chicken stock
2 1/2 cups milk
Two 6-oz. cans crabmeat, drained
12-oz. can corn kernels, drained
Salt and ground black pepper
2 tbsp. chopped fresh parsley

Heat the oil in a large saucepan. Add the onion, garlic, and chili, and cook gently for 4 minutes. Stir in the potatoes, pepper, and stock, and bring to a boil. Reduce the heat, cover, and simmer for about 5 minutes, until the potatoes are tender.

Process half the soup until smooth in a food processor or blender. Add the milk, crabmeat, and corn to the pan, and heat through. Then return the puréed soup to the pan. Add salt and pepper to taste. Stir in the parsley and serve.

Serves 4

cappelletti in brodo

see variations page 161

This classic Italian soup of filled pasta in broth is traditionally served on New Year's Day, but it's the perfect choice any time you need an almost-instant bowl of soup.

5 cups chicken stock
4 oz. cappelletti
4 tbsp. white wine

2 tbsp. chopped fresh parsley
Salt and ground black pepper
Parmesan cheese shavings, to serve

Bring the stock to the boil in a large saucepan. Add the pasta and cook according to the package instructions, until al dente, tender with a bit of bite (not soft).

Stir in the wine, parsley, and salt and pepper to taste. Ladle the soup into bowls and serve sprinkled with Parmesan shavings.

Serves 4

fresh vegetable minestrone

see variations page 162

Simple, healthy minestrone makes a great lunch or dinner. Vary the choice of vegetables, if you like, according to what is good and is in season.

2 tbsp. olive oil
1 onion, finely chopped
2 garlic cloves, crushed
1 carrot, quartered and sliced
1 zucchini, quartered and sliced
1/4 small green cabbage, shredded

4 ripe tomatoes, peeled and chopped
1 tbsp. sun-dried tomato paste
5 cups vegetable stock
4 oz. angel hair pasta or vermicelli, broken into
     short lengths
Salt and ground black pepper

Heat the oil in a large saucepan. Add the onion and garlic, and cook gently for 4 minutes. Add the carrot, zucchini, cabbage, tomatoes, tomato paste, and stock. Bring to a boil, reduce the heat, cover, and simmer gently for 4 minutes.

Add the pasta and simmer for about 2 minutes more, until the pasta is al dente, tender with a bit of bite (not soft). Add salt and pepper to taste and serve.

Serves 4

cream of tomato soup

see variations page 163

Such a classic and so incredibly easy to make — you can whip up a pan of this delicious soup in no time. Serve it as as an elegant appetizer or as a simple lunch with crusty bread.

2 tbsp. olive oil
1 onion, chopped
3 garlic cloves, crushed
Two 14-oz. cans chopped tomatoes
2 1/2 cups vegetable stock

2 handfuls fresh basil, plus extra leaves
    to garnish
1/2 cup heavy cream
About 1/4 tsp. superfine sugar
Salt and ground black pepper

Heat the oil in a large saucepan. Add the onion and garlic, and cook gently for 4 minutes. Stir in the tomatoes and stock, and bring to a boil. Then reduce the heat, cover, and simmer for 10 minutes.

Pour the soup into a food processor or blender, add the basil and blend until smooth. Return the soup to the pan, stir in about two-thirds of the cream, and warm through without boiling. Stir in sugar, salt and pepper to taste.

Ladle the soup into bowls and serve drizzled with the remaining cream, and garnish with a few fresh basil leaves.

Serves 4

spring leaf soup

see variations page 164

Tender spring leaves take only minutes to cook and taste delicious blended into a refreshing, green soup.

1 large potato, diced
3 3/4 cups vegetable stock
2 bunches scallions, sliced
3 large handfuls spinach, roughly shredded
2 large handfuls arugula, roughly shredded
2 large handfuls sorrel, roughly shredded

Generous 3/4 cup white wine
1/2 cup heavy cream, plus extra for serving (optional)
Salt and ground black pepper
Finely shredded spinach or sorrel, to garnish

Put the potato and stock in a large saucepan. Bring to a boil, then reduce the heat, cover and simmer for about 5 minutes, until the potato is tender. Add the scallions, spinach, arugula, and sorrel. Cover and simmer for 2 to 3 minutes, until the leaves are wilted.

Pour the soup into a food processor or blender and process to a smooth purée. Return to the pan, stir in the wine and cream, and warm through. Add salt and pepper to taste and serve ladled into bowls. Drizzle with a little extra cream, if desired, and garnish with finely shredded spinach or sorrel.

Serves 4

asian-style shrimp & noodle broth

see variations page 165

You can use any noodles you like for this broth — fine rice or soba (wheat) noodles work particularly well.

2 tbsp. sunflower oil
3 shallots, finely chopped
2 tsp. grated fresh ginger
1 green chili, seeded and finely chopped
2 tsp. Thai green curry paste
5 cups vegetable stock
6–8 oz. noodles

2 tsp. brown sugar
Juice of about 1/2 lime, to taste
8 oz. peeled cooked tiger shrimp
4 handfuls beansprouts
1 bunch scallions, sliced at an angle
Large handful of fresh cilantro leaves, plus
    extra to garnish

Heat the oil in a large saucepan. Add the shallots, ginger, chili, and curry paste, and cook gently for 2 minutes. Stir in the stock, bring to a boil, cover, and simmer for 10 minutes. Meanwhile, cook the noodles in a separate pan of boiling water according to the package instructions. Drain and set aside.

Stir the sugar and lime juice into the broth. Add the shrimp and cooked noodles, and warm through. Add the beansprouts and scallions, and stir in the cilantro. Ladle the soup into bowls, garnish with extra cilantro, and serve immediately.

Serves 4

cream of chicken & saffron soup

see variations page 166

Incredibly quick and easy to make, yet luxurious and sophisticated, this soup makes a perfect speedy appetizer for an elegant dinner.

2 tbsp. olive oil
1 onion, finely chopped
2 garlic cloves, crushed
12 oz. skinless, boneless cooked chicken,
    cut into small bite-size pieces
3 1/2 cups chicken stock

Generous 3/4 cup white wine
Good pinch of saffron threads
Generous 3/4 cup heavy cream
Salt and ground black pepper
2 tbsp. snipped fresh chives

Heat the oil in a large saucepan. Add the onion and garlic, and cook for 5 minutes. Add the chicken, stock, and wine, and bring to a boil. Reduce the heat, cover the pan, and simmer for 5 minutes. Stir in the saffron and cook for 1 minute.

Remove the pan from the heat and stir in the cream. Season to taste with salt and pepper, then ladle the soup into bowls. Serve sprinkled with chives.

Serves 4

celery soup with sherry

see variations page 167

Sherry brings an interesting edge to the flavor of this smooth, creamy soup, studded with chunks of tender, mild celery.

1 head of celery
3 tbsp. butter
1 onion, finely chopped
2 tbsp. all-purpose flour
4 1/4 cups chicken or vegetable stock

3/4 cup sherry
1/2 cup heavy cream
2 tbsp. chopped fresh parsley
Salt and ground black pepper

Cut 1 celery stalk into short fine sticks and set aside for garnishing the soup. Thinly slice the remaining celery and set aside.

Melt the butter in a large saucepan. Add the onion and cook gently for 4 minutes. Stir in the flour and cook for 1 minute, then gradually stir in the stock. Add the sliced celery and bring to a boil. Then reduce the heat, cover the pan, and simmer for about 10 minutes, until the celery is tender.

Pour half the soup into a food processor or blender and process until smooth, then return it to the pan. Stir in the sherry, cream, and parsley, and warm through without boiling. Add salt and pepper to taste, and serve garnished with celery.

Serves 4

variations

broccoli soup with parmesan toasts

see base recipe page 139

cauliflower soup with parmesan toasts
Prepare the basic recipe, using cauliflower in place of the broccoli.

broccoli & cauliflower soup with parmesan toasts
Prepare the basic recipe, using 8 oz. broccoli and 8 oz. cauliflower.

chunky broccoli soup with parmesan toasts
Prepare the basic recipe, removing about a fourth of the cooked broccoli florets from the pan before processing the soup. Return the broccoli florets to the pan with the milk and nutmeg.

broccoli & spinach soup with parmesan toasts
Prepare the basic recipe, using 12 oz. broccoli and 8 oz. spinach. Add the spinach about 4 minutes after the broccoli.

zucchini & broccoli soup with parmesan toasts
Prepare the basic recipe, using 8 oz. zucchini and 12 oz. broccoli.

spiced chickpea & lemon soup

see base recipe page 141

spiced borlotti bean & lemon soup
Prepare the basic recipe, using borlotti beans in place of the chickpeas.

spiced navy bean & lemon soup
Prepare the basic recipe, using navy beans in place of the chickpeas.

spiced chickpea & lemon soup with fresh cilantro
Prepare the basic recipe, using chopped fresh cilantro in place of
the parsley.

spiced cannellini bean & lemon soup
Prepare the basic recipe, using cannellini beans in place of the chickpeas.

fiery chickpea & lemon soup
Prepare the basic recipe, stirring in 1/2 teaspoon crushed dried red chilies
with the spices.

variations

crab & corn chowder

see base recipe page 142

crab & corn chowder with scallions
Prepare the basic recipe, stirring in 4 sliced scallions in place of the parsley.

crab, corn & green bell pepper chowder
Prepare the basic recipe, adding 1 seeded, finely chopped green bell pepper in place of the red bell pepper.

tuna & corn chowder
Prepare the basic recipe, adding two 6-oz. cans tuna fish, drained, in place of the crabmeat.

mussel & corn chowder
Prepare the basic recipe, using 12 oz. cooked, shelled mussels in place of the crabmeat.

shrimp & corn chowder
Prepare the basic recipe, using 12 oz. peeled, cooked shrimp in place of the crabmeat.

variations

cappelletti in brodo

see base recipe page 145

cappelletti in brodo with chicken
Prepare the basic recipe, adding 1 shredded, cooked, skinless chicken breast to the broth.

cappelletti in brodo with roast peppers
Prepare the basic recipe, adding 3 sliced, bottled roasted bell peppers to the broth.

ravioli in brodo
Prepare the basic recipe, using mushroom ravioli in place of the cappelletti, and vegetable stock in place of the chicken stock.

cappelletti in brodo with beans
Prepare the basic recipe, adding a 14-oz. can drained, rinsed borlotti or navy beans to the broth.

variations

fresh vegetable minestrone

see base recipe page 146

fresh vegetable minestrone with pesto
Prepare the basic recipe and serve topped with a spoonful of pesto.

fresh vegetable minestrone with green beans
Prepare the basic recipe, adding 4 oz. green beans, cut into 1-inch lengths, in place of the zucchini.

fresh vegetable minestrone with navy beans
Prepare the basic recipe, adding a 14-oz. can drained, rinsed navy beans with the vegetables.

fresh vegetable minestrone with bacon
Prepare the basic recipe, frying 3 roughly chopped, bacon slices with the onion and garlic.

fresh vegetable minestrone with chicken
Prepare the basic recipe, adding 1 shredded, skinless, cooked chicken breast with the vegetables, and using chicken stock in place of the vegetable stock.

variations

cream of tomato soup

see base recipe page 149

cream of tomato & bell pepper soup
Prepare the basic recipe, adding 2 seeded, chopped red bell peppers with the tomatoes.

red-hot cream of tomato soup
Prepare the basic recipe, frying 2 seeded, chopped red chilies with the onion and garlic.

cream of tomato soup with fresh cilantro
Prepare the basic recipe, using fresh cilantro in place of the basil.

cream of tomato soup with fresh mint
Prepare the basic recipe, using 1 tablespoon chopped fresh mint in place of the basil, and garnishing with fresh mint leaves.

fresh tomato soup
Prepare the basic recipe, using 6 peeled, chopped ripe tomatoes in place of canned tomatoes.

variations

spring leaf soup

see base recipe page 150

spinach & arugula soup
Prepare the basic recipe, using 3 large handfuls each of spinach and arugula, and omitting the sorrel.

spring leaf soup with artichoke bruschetta
Prepare the basic recipe. Serve with artichoke bruschetta: Toast 8 slices of baguette until golden on both sides, then spread each with a little pesto and top with a bottled marinated artichoke heart.

spring leaf soup with red onion
Prepare the basic recipe, using 1 finely chopped red onion in place of the scallions. Serve garnished with more chopped red onion.

spring leaf & watercress soup
Prepare the basic recipe, adding a large handful of shredded watercress with the other leaves.

variations

asian-style shrimp & noodle broth

see base recipe page 153

asian-style chicken & noodle broth
Prepare the basic recipe, using chicken stock in place of the vegetable stock, and adding 2 shredded, skinless cooked chicken breasts in place of the shrimp.

asian-style shrimp & noodle broth with coconut milk
Prepare the basic recipe using 3 1/2 cups stock and 1 3/4 cups coconut milk.

asian-style shrimp & noodle broth with fresh basil
Prepare the basic recipe, using fresh basil in place of the cilantro.

asian-style shrimp & noodle broth with fresh mint
Prepare the basic recipe, using 1 tablespoon chopped fresh mint in place of the cilantro, and fresh mint leaves to garnish.

variations

cream of chicken & saffron soup

see base recipe page 154

cream of chicken & saffron soup with tomatoes
Prepare the basic recipe, adding 3 peeled, seeded, and chopped tomatoes with the stock.

cream of chicken & saffron soup with parsley
Prepare the basic soup, using parsley in place of the chives.

cream of chicken & saffron soup with scallions
Prepare the basic soup, stirring in 1 bunch sliced scallions with the saffron threads.

spiced cream of chicken & saffron soup
Prepare the basic soup, frying 1 chopped, seeded fresh red chili with the onions and garlic.

celery soup with sherry

see base recipe page 157

celery soup with white wine
Prepare the basic recipe, using white wine in place of the sherry.

celery & chicken soup with sherry
Prepare the basic recipe, adding 2 skinless cooked chicken breasts, cut into bite-size pieces, with the celery.

celery & turkey soup with sherry
Prepare the basic recipe, adding 8–12 oz. cooked turkey meat, cut into bite-size pieces, with the celery.

celery & tomato soup with sherry
Prepare the basic soup, adding 3 peeled, seeded, and chopped tomatoes with the celery.

fennel soup with sherry
Prepare the basic recipe, using 2 sliced fennel bulbs in place of the celery.

hot & spicy

Hot chilies and warm spices bring punchy flavor
to all types of soups from all over the world. Every
country has its signature soup, so take your pick
from the hot and peppery or warm and spicy
recipes presented in this chapter.

moroccan harira

see variations page 188

There are countless variations of this soup, which is served in the evening during the 30-day fast of Ramadan. This recipe, with lentils and chicken, is spiced, but not too hot.

1/2 cup Puy lentils, or brown
    or green lentils
2 tbsp. olive oil
1 onion, finely chopped
2 garlic cloves, crushed
1/2 tsp. ground ginger
2 tsp. ground cinnamon
1/2 tsp. ground turmeric
1 tsp. harissa (hot chili paste)

5 cups chicken stock
14-oz. can chopped tomatoes
1 tbsp. tomato paste
14-oz. can chickpeas, drained
2 skinless boneless chicken breasts, cut into
    bite-size strips
Juice of 1/4 to 1/2 lemon
Salt and ground black pepper
Handful of fresh cilantro, chopped, for garnish

Cook the lentils in plenty of boiling water for 25 minutes. Drain and set aside. Heat the oil in a large saucepan. Add the onions and garlic, and cook gently for 5 minutes. Stir in the ginger, cinnamon, turmeric, and harissa, then pour in the stock. Add the tomatoes, tomato paste, chickpeas, and cooked lentils.

Bring the soup to a boil, reduce the heat, and cover. Cook for about 15 minutes. Add the chicken and cook for a further 5 to 10 minutes, until the chicken is cooked through. Squeeze in lemon juice and salt and pepper to taste. Serve topped with chopped fresh cilantro.

Serves 4

curried parsnip soup

see variations page 189

This hearty, warming winter soup is a real classic. Sweet, fragrant parsnips go wonderfully with Indian-style spicing. You can serve with any bread, but wedges of naan complement the Indian flavor.

2 tbsp. sunflower oil
3 garlic cloves, crushed
1 onion, chopped
2 green chilies, seeded and chopped
1 tsp. ground cumin
1 tsp. ground coriander
1/2 tsp. ground ginger

1/2 tsp. ground turmeric
5 parsnips, peeled and chopped
5 cups vegetable or chicken stock
Juice of about 1/2 lemon, to taste
Salt and ground black pepper
Plain yogurt and wedges of naan bread, to serve
1 tbsp. chopped fresh mint, to garnish

Heat the oil in a large saucepan. Add the garlic, onion, and chilies, and cook gently for about 4 minutes. Stir in the cumin, coriander, ginger, turmeric, and parsnips, then pour in the stock. Bring to a boil and reduce the heat. Simmer the soup for about 20 minutes, until the parsnips are tender.

Process the soup in a food processor or blender until smooth. Stir in lemon juice and salt and pepper to taste. Serve the soup topped with a little yogurt and sprinkled with mint, with wedges of naan bread on the side.

Serves 4

indian-inspired mulligatawny

see variations page 190

Created in the time of the Raj, this creamy lentil soup enriched with coconut milk takes its name from a Tamil phrase "milagu thanni," meaning pepper water.

2 tbsp. sunflower oil
1 onion, finely chopped
3 garlic cloves, crushed
2 hot green chilies, seeded and chopped
2 tsp. ground cumin
1 tsp. ground coriander
1 tsp. ground turmeric
1/2 tsp. ground cinnamon
4 1/4 cups vegetable stock

1 3/4 cups coconut milk
Generous 1/2 cup red lentils
2 celery stalks, chopped
2 carrots, chopped
1 apple, chopped
Juice of about 1/4 lemon, to taste
Salt and ground black pepper
Handful of fresh cilantro leaves

Heat the oil in a large saucepan. Add the onion and garlic, and cook for about 4 minutes. Stir in the chilies, cumin, coriander, turmeric, and cinnamon, followed by the stock, coconut milk, lentils, celery, carrots, and apple. Bring to a boil, then reduce the heat, cover, and simmer for about 30 minutes, until the lentils are tender.

Stir in lemon juice and salt and pepper to taste. Ladle the soup into serving bowls and sprinkle with fresh cilantro.

Serves 4

spiced carrot soup

see variations page 191

Inspired by the flavors of Morocco, this spiced carrot soup is delicious with wedges of toasted pita bread or Middle-Eastern flatbread as a meal, or on its own as an appetizer.

2 tbsp. sunflower oil
1 onion, chopped
3 garlic cloves, crushed
2 tsp. ground cumin
1 tsp. ground coriander
1/2 tsp. ground ginger
1 tsp. paprika
Generous pinch of cayenne pepper

1 small potato, diced
1 lb. carrots, sliced
5 cups vegetable or chicken stock
Juice of 1 orange
1 to 1 1/2 tbsp. red wine vinegar
Salt and ground black pepper
Handful of fresh cilantro, chopped

Heat the oil in a large saucepan. Add the onion and garlic, and cook gently for 4 minutes. Stir in the cumin, coriander, ginger, paprika, and cayenne pepper, then add the potato, carrots, and stock.

Bring to a boil, reduce the heat, and cover the pan. Simmer for about 20 minutes, until the vegetables are tender. Process the soup in a food processor or blender until smooth. Stir in the orange juice, then add vinegar, salt and pepper to taste. Ladle the soup into bowls, sprinkle with cilantro, and serve.

Serves 4

roasted squash soup with coconut milk & thai spices

see variations page 192

Sweet, tender roasted squash, fragrant Thai spices, and creamy coconut milk make a delicious combination in this chunky soup.

1 butternut squash, seeded, peeled, and cut
    into chunks
3 tbsp. sunflower oil
2 shallots, finely chopped
2 garlic cloves, crushed
2 tsp. grated fresh ginger
2 green chilies, seeded and shredded, plus extra
    to garnish

2 lemongrass stalks, chopped
4 kaffir lime leaves, shredded
3 1/2 cups vegetable stock
1 3/4 cups coconut milk
Juice of about 1 lime
1 tbsp. fish sauce
Handful of fresh cilantro leaves

Preheat the oven to 400°F (200°C). Put the squash in a baking dish, drizzle 1 tablespoon of the oil over all, and toss to coat. Roast for about 25 minutes, until tender.

Heat the remaining oil in a large saucepan. Add the shallots, garlic, and ginger, and cook gently for about 3 minutes. Add the chilies, lemongrass, lime leaves, stock, and coconut milk, and bring to a boil. Reduce the heat, cover, and simmer for about 20 minutes. Add the roasted squash to the soup, then stir in lime juice and fish sauce to taste. Serve ladled into bowls, sprinkled with fresh cilantro.

Serves 4

hot chili-squid soup

see variations page 193

Chilies, tomatoes, and squid seem to be a partnership made in heaven, and they are divine in this light tomato broth.

6 squid, cleaned
Juice of 1 lemon
3 tbsp. olive oil
3 shallots, finely chopped
2 hot red chilies, seeded and chopped
1 lb. ripe tomatoes, peeled, seeded and chopped

5 cups fish or vegetable stock
1 tbsp. tomato paste
1/2 tsp. ground cinnamon
Pinch of light brown sugar
Salt and ground black pepper
1 tbsp. chopped fresh mint

Separate the tentacles from the squid in one piece. Discard the head. Slice the bodies into rings and put in a bowl with the tentacles and lemon juice. Cover and chill for 30 minutes.

Heat 2 tablespoons of the oil in a large saucepan. Add the shallots and chilies, and cook gently for 2 minutes. Add the tomatoes, stock, tomato paste, and cinnamon. Bring to a boil, reduce heat, cover, and simmer for 10 minutes. Process the soup in a blender until smooth, then return it to the pan. Add sugar and salt and pepper to taste; keep warm.

Drain the squid, pat dry on paper towels, then season with salt and pepper. Heat the remaining oil in a nonstick skillet. Fry the squid for 1 minute, until just cooked. Ladle the soup into bowls, spoon the squid on top, sprinkle with fresh mint, and serve.

Serves 4

spicy chicken gumbo soup

see variations page 194

This classic cross between stew and soup is traditionally served ladled over cooked rice to make a substantial meal. Serve it without rice for a lighter lunch.

2 tbsp. olive oil
1 onion, chopped
2 garlic cloves, finely chopped
1 1/2 tbsp. all-purpose flour
5 cups chicken stock
2 green bell peppers, seeded and chopped
1 1/2 lb. okra, trimmed and cut into
    1/2-in. slices
4 ripe tomatoes, peeled and chopped

2 tbsp. tomato paste
1 tsp. fresh thyme
1 tsp. cayenne pepper
2 cooked skinless chicken breasts, cut into
    bite-size pieces
1 cup corn
Salt and ground black pepper
Tabasco sauce, to taste
Prepared rice, to serve

Heat the oil in a large saucepan. Add the onion and garlic, and cook gently for about 4 minutes. Stir in the flour and cook for another minute. Gradually stir in the chicken stock, followed by the peppers, okra, tomatoes, tomato paste, thyme, and cayenne pepper. Bring the soup to a boil, then reduce the heat, cover, and simmer for about 30 minutes, stirring occasionally.

Stir in the chicken and corn, and cook for a further 30 minutes, stirring occasionally. Add salt and pepper, and Tabasco sauce to taste. Serve the soup ladled over rice.

Serves 4

spicy cauliflower & potato soup

see variations page 195

Coconut and Indian-style spice mixtures taste terrific with the cauliflower and potatoes in this chunky soup.

2 tbsp. sunflower oil
1 onion, finely chopped
2 green chilies, seeded and chopped
2 garlic cloves, finely chopped
2 tsp. grated fresh ginger
2 tsp. ground cumin
1 tsp. ground coriander
1/2 tsp. ground turmeric

3 1/2 cups vegetable or chicken stock
1 3/4 cups coconut milk
1 large potato, peeled and cut into cubes
1 small cauliflower, broken into bite-size florets
Salt and ground black pepper
Juice of about 1/2 lemon, to taste
Handful of fresh cilantro, chopped

Heat the oil in a saucepan. Add the onion, chilies, garlic, and ginger, and cook for 4 minutes. Stir in the cumin, coriander, and turmeric. Add the stock, coconut milk, potatoes, and cauliflower. Bring to a boil, reduce the heat, cover and simmer gently for 10 to 15 minutes.

When the vegetables are tender, ladle half of them into a blender or food processor and process until smooth, then stir this purée back into the soup. Add salt, pepper, and lemon juice to taste. Ladle the soup into bowls, sprinkle with fresh cilantro, and serve.

Serves 4

red-hot spicy chickpea & pasta soup

see variations page 196

This chunky, wholesome soup has a real bite — making it perfect for serving on a cold day when you really need to warm yourself up.

2 tbsp. olive oil
3 red chilies, seeded and chopped
3 garlic cloves, crushed
6 ripe tomatoes, peeled and chopped
4 1/4 cups vegetable or chicken stock
14-oz. can chickpeas, drained and rinsed

4 oz. small pasta shapes
Bunch of scallions, sliced
1 tbsp. chopped fresh mint
Salt
Parmesan cheese shavings, to serve

Heat the oil in a large saucepan. Add the chilies and garlic, and cook gently for 2 minutes. Stir in the tomatoes, stock, and chickpeas, and bring to a boil. Reduce the heat, cover, and simmer for about 20 minutes.

Add the pasta to the soup and simmer for another 5 minutes, until tender. Stir in the scallions, mint, and salt to taste. Ladle the soup into bowls and serve immediately, sprinkled with Parmesan shavings.

Serves 4

ginger & tiger shrimp soup

see variations page 197

Tender juicy shrimp cooked in a fragrant broth and served with rice noodles taste divine and couldn't be easier to prepare.

2 tbsp. sunflower oil
2 tsp. grated fresh ginger
2 garlic cloves, crushed
2 shallots, finely chopped
5 cups fish or vegetable stock
2 tbsp. sweet chili sauce
4 oz. rice noodles

Juice of 1/2 to 1 lime, to taste
1 tsp. Thai fish sauce
8–12 oz. tiger shrimp, peeled
    and deveined
Bunch of scallions, sliced
Handful of fresh basil leaves, torn

Heat the oil in a large saucepan. Add the ginger, garlic, and shallots, and cook for 2 minutes. Pour in the stock and chili sauce, and bring to a boil. Reduce the heat, cover, and simmer for about 20 minutes.

Toward the end of the cooking time, put the noodles in a medium bowl, pour boiling water over them and leave to soak for 5 minutes, until tender (following the package instructions). Drain and set aside.

Stir in lime juice and fish sauce to taste. Add the shrimp and cook for about 2 minutes, until the shrimp are pink and cooked through. Stir in the scallions and noodles. Ladle the soup into bowls, sprinke with the basil, and serve immediately.

Serves 4

moroccan harira

see base recipe page 169

vegetarian harira

Prepare the basic recipe, using vegetable stock in place of the chicken stock and omitting the chicken.

lamb harira

Prepare the basic recipe, using lamb or beef stock in place of the chicken stock, and 3/4 cup cooked lamb in place of the chicken.

mixed vegetable harira

Prepare the basic recipe, adding 1 zucchini, cut into fourths lengthwise and sliced, 1 carrot, cut into fourths lengthwise and sliced, and 1 finely diced red bell pepper with the chickpeas and chicken.

fiery harira

Prepare the basic recipe, adding 1/4 to 1/2 teaspoon crushed dried red chili with the spices.

curried parsnip soup

see base recipe page 171

curried carrot soup
Prepare the basic recipe, using 5 large carrots and 1 small potato in place of the parsnips.

simple curried parsnip soup
Prepare the basic recipe, using 1 1/2 tablespoons curry paste in place of the cumin, coriander, ginger, and turmeric.

curried beet soup
Prepare the basic recipe, using 5 large peeled, chopped, raw beets in place of the parsnips.

curried parsnip & carrot soup
Prepare the basic recipe, using 3 parsnips and 3 large carrots.

variations

indian-inspired mulligatawny

see base recipe page 172

mulligatawny with chicken
Prepare the basic recipe, using chicken stock in place of the vegetable stock. Add 2 shredded, skinless cooked chicken breasts toward the end of cooking.

indian-inspired mulligatawny with lamb
Prepare the basic recipe, using lamb stock in place of the vegetable stock. Add 3/4 cup shredded cooked lamb toward the end of cooking.

indian-inspired mulligatawny with tomatoes
Prepare the basic recipe, adding 4 ripe, peeled, chopped tomatoes with the other vegetables.

indian-inspired low-fat mulligatawny
Prepare the basic recipe, using 5 cups vegetable stock and omitting the coconut milk. Serve topped with a swirl of low-fat plain yogurt.

indian-inspired mulligatawny with fresh mint
Prepare the basic recipe, sprinkling the finished soup with a little chopped fresh mint in place of the cilantro.

spiced carrot soup

see base recipe page 175

chilled spiced carrot soup
Prepare the basic recipe, then leave to cool and chill for at least 4 hours
before serving.

spiced carrot soup with harissa
Prepare the basic recipe, adding 1 teaspoon harissa (hot chili paste) in place
of the paprika and cayenne pepper.

spiced carrot soup with mint
Prepare the basic recipe, sprinkling the soup with chopped fresh mint
instead of cilantro.

spiced carrot soup with sour cream
Prepare the basic recipe and serve each portion topped with a spoonful
of sour cream.

spiced carrot & red pepper soup
Prepare the basic recipe, using 1 lb. carrots and 2 seeded, diced
red bell peppers.

variations

roasted squash soup with coconut milk & thai spices

see base recipe page 176

roasted squash soup with coconut milk, thai spices & toasted cashew nuts
Prepare the basic recipe, scattering toasted cashew nuts over the soup to serve.

velvet-smooth roasted squash soup with coconut milk & thai spices
Prepare the basic recipe and process until smooth in a blender or food processor before serving.

roasted squash & shrimp soup with coconut milk & thai spices
Prepare the basic recipe, adding 20 peeled, cooked tiger shrimp to the soup with the squash.

roasted squash & chicken soup with coconut milk & thai spices
Prepare the basic recipe, adding 2 cooked chicken breasts, cut into bite-size pieces, with the squash.

roasted squash soup with noodles, coconut milk, & thai spices
Prepare the basic recipe, and serve ladled over freshly cooked noodles.

hot chili–squid soup

see base recipe page 179

chunky hot chili–squid soup
Prepare the basic recipe, but do not blend the soup — serve it chunky, topped with the squid and mint.

hot chili–squid soup with cilantro
Prepare the basic recipe, sprinkling the soup with chopped fresh cilantro in place of the mint.

garlick chili–squid soup
Prepare the basic recipe, using 3 crushed garlic cloves in place of the shallots. Sauté the garlic with the chili for about 1 minute, then add the tomatoes and stock, and continue as in the basic recipe.

tomato & ginger soup with squid
Prepare the basic recipe, using 2 teaspoons grated fresh ginger in place of the chilies.

spicy chicken gumbo soup

see base recipe page 180

vegetarian spicy gumbo soup
Prepare the basic recipe, using vegetable stock in place of the chicken stock, and omitting the chicken.

spicy chicken gumbo soup with green beans
Prepare the basic recipe. About 10 minutes before the end of the cooking time, stir in 4 oz. trimmed green beans cut into 1-inch lengths.

green chili chicken gumbo soup
Prepare the basic recipe, sautéing 2 seeded, chopped green chilies with the onion and garlic. Use half the amount of cayenne pepper.

spicy chicken gumbo with fresh mint
Prepare the basic recipe, sprinkling the soup with chopped fresh mint before serving.

spicy cauliflower & potato soup

see base recipe page 183

smooth spicy cauliflower & potato soup
Prepare the basic recipe and process the whole batch of soup until smooth
before serving.

spicy cauliflower, potato & chickpea soup
Prepare the basic recipe, using half the quantity of potato and adding
a 14-oz. can drained, rinsed, chickpeas with the potato and cauliflower.

spicy cauliflower & potato soup with naan
Prepare the basic recipe and serve the soup with wedges of naan bread.

spicy cauliflower & potato soup with yogurt & mango chutney
Prepare the basic recipe and serve bowls of soup topped with a spoonful
of plain yogurt and a dollop of mango chutney.

spicy cauliflower & carrot soup
Prepare the basic recipe, using 4 carrots in place of the potatoes.

red-hot spicy chickpea & pasta soup

see base recipe page 184

red-hot kidney bean & pasta soup
Prepare the basic recipe, using kidney beans in place of the chickpeas.

red-hot chickpea & vermicelli soup
Prepare the basic recipe, using vermicelli in place of the soup pasta.

red-hot navy bean & pasta soup
Prepare the basic recipe, using navy beans in place of the chickpeas.

green hot chickpea & pasta soup
Prepare the basic recipe, using green chilies in place of red.

red-hot chickpea & pasta soup with bacon
Prepare the basic recipe, frying 2 roughly chopped, bacon slices with the chili and garlic.

ginger & tiger shrimp soup

see base recipe page 187

ginger & salmon soup
Prepare the basic recipe, omitting the shrimp. Broil 4 (5 oz.) portions of
salmon fillets while the soup cooks. Place the noodles in bowls, top with
the salmon, and ladle over the broth.

spicy ginger & tiger shrimp soup
Prepare the basic recipe, frying 1 seeded, chopped red chili with the ginger,
garlic, and shallots.

fragrant ginger & tiger shrimp soup
Prepare the basic recipe, adding 2 chopped lemongrass stalks with the stock,
and sprinkling the finished soup with a handful of cilantro leaves in place
of the basil.

ginger & tiger shrimp soup with chives
Prepare the basic recipe, sprinkling 1/2 tablespoon snipped fresh chives over
each bowl of soup in place of the basil.

ginger & tiger shrimp soup with fresh mint
Prepare the basic recipe, sprinkling 1 teaspoon chopped fresh mint over each
bowl of soup in place of the basil.

sophisticated starters

When you're planning a special meal, a bowl of

cleverly garnished soup is ideal for setting the style

in the first course. Serve any one of the stunning

soups in this chapter and you will feel like the "host

with the most."

spiced cherry tomato & vodka soup with seared scallops

see variations page 216

Sweet, tender seared scallops marinated in ginger and lime are a real gourmet treat — perfect for dressing up a simple tomato soup.

2 tbsp. sunflower oil, plus extra for frying
2 shallots, finely chopped
2 garlic cloves, crushed
2 hot red chilies, seeded and finely chopped
1 lb. cherry tomatoes
4 1/4 cups vegetable stock

1 tsp. grated fresh ginger
Juice of 1 lime
1 tsp. chopped fresh mint, plus extra to garnish
Salt
12 scallops, shelled and cleaned
2 tbsp. vodka

Heat the oil in a large saucepan. Add the shallots, garlic, and chilies. Cook for 2 minutes. Add the tomatoes and stock. Bring to a boil, reduce the heat, cover, and simmer for 10 minutes.

In a separate bowl combine the ginger, lime juice, mint, and a pinch of salt, and pour onto the scallops. Set aside until the soup is cooked. Process the soup in a blender until smooth, then strain it back into the rinsed-out pan. Add salt and keep warm.

Heat a nonstick skillet. Add a drizzle of oil. Add the scallops and marinade, and sear on each side for 1 minute, until just cooked. Stir the vodka into the soup and ladle it into bowls. Pile three scallops in the center of each portion. Sprinkle with a little mint and serve.

Serves 4

garden pea soup with prosciutto croûtes

see variations page 217

Frozen peas that are frozen almost as soon as they are picked often have a better flavor than fresh vegetables, and they are perfect in this luxurious, yet simple, soup.

2 tbsp. olive oil
2 shallots, chopped
1 garlic clove, crushed
Two 10 oz. packages frozen peas
3 cups vegetable or chicken stock
1/4 cup heavy cream
Salt and ground black pepper

for the croûtes

2 tbsp. good-quality mayonnaise
1/4 tsp. Dijon mustard
1/4 tsp. grated lemon zest
4 small slices baguette
2 strips prosciutto, halved

Heat the oil in a large saucepan. Add the shallots and garlic, and cook gently for about 2 minutes. Add the peas and stock, and bring to a boil. Remove from the heat and process the soup in a food processor or blender until smooth. Stir in the cream and season with salt and pepper to taste.

Meanwhile, prepare the croûtes. Combine the mayonnaise, mustard, and lemon zest. Toast the bread slices on both sides until golden, then leave to cool. To serve, ladle the soup into bowls. Top each toast with a dollop of mayonnaise and curl a strip of prosciutto on top. Grind a little black pepper over the top and serve with the soup.

Serves 4

spicy crab & coconut soup

see variations page 218

Choose red-hot bird's eye chilies to add a real bite to this rich, creamy soup with its delicious chunks of crabmeat. Small bowlfuls are ample for an appetizer.

2 tbsp. sunflower oil
3 shallots, finely chopped
2 tsp. grated fresh ginger
2 lemongrass stalks, chopped
2 green chilies, seeded and finely chopped
4 1/4 cups vegetable stock

1/2 cup coconut cream
4 scallions, sliced
Two 6-oz. cans crabmeat
Juice of 1/4 to 1/2 lime, to taste
Salt and ground black pepper
Handful of fresh cilantro leaves, chopped

Heat the oil in a large saucepan. Add the shallots, ginger, lemongrass, and chilies, and cook gently for about 2 minutes. Pour in the stock and bring to a boil. Reduce the heat, cover, and simmer the soup gently for about 20 minutes.

Stir in the coconut cream, then add the scallions and crabmeat. Warm the soup, without allowing it to boil, for about 2 minutes. Add lime juice, and salt and pepper to taste. Ladle the soup into bowls, sprinkle with fresh cilantro, and serve.

Serves 4

fava bean & sugar snap soup

see variations page 219

Light and fresh, this is a lovely soup to make in summer, when fava beans and sugar snap peas are in abundance and at their best.

2 tbsp. olive oil
2 shallots, finely chopped
2 garlic cloves, crushed
6 ripe tomatoes, peeled and chopped
5 cups vegetable stock

1 lb. fava beans, shelled
8 oz. sugarsnap peas, sliced
Handful of fresh basil leaves, torn
Salt and ground black pepper

Heat the oil in a large saucepan. Add the shallots and garlic, and cook gently, stirring occasionally, for 2 to 3 minutes. Add the tomatoes and stock, and bring to a boil. Reduce the heat, cover, and simmer gently for 10 minutes.

Add the beans and sugar snap peas to the soup. Simmer for about 3 minutes, until the vegetables are just tender, but still with a crisp bite. Add the basil and salt and pepper to taste, then serve the soup ladled into bowls.

Serves 4

creamed artichoke soup with anchovy toasts

see variations page 220

There's something rather special about artichokes, and this simple soup, made using canned artichoke hearts, takes all the hassle out of the preparation.

2 tbsp. olive oil, plus extra
 for drizzling
1 onion, chopped
3 garlic cloves, chopped
2 tsp. ground cumin
Two 14-oz. cans artichoke hearts,
 drained
5 cups vegetable stock

2 tsp. chopped fresh mint, plus extra to garnish
Salt and ground black pepper

for the anchovy toasts

4 anchovies
1/4 cup (1/2 stick) butter, at room temperature
8 slices baguette

Heat the oil in a large saucepan. Add the onion and garlic, and cook gently for 4 minutes. Stir in the cumin, then add the artichoke hearts and stock. Bring to a boil, reduce the heat, and cover the pan. Simmer the soup for 10 minutes, then process it in a food processor or blender until smooth. Stir in the mint and check the seasoning.

Crush the anchovies with a spoon, then beat in the butter. Toast the bread on both sides, spread with anchovy butter, and season with black pepper. Ladle the soup into bowls, sprinkle with mint, and float a toast in each portion; offer the remaining toasts on the side.

Serves 4

vermouth & fennel soup

see variations page 221

Vermouth, with its herblike aroma, is a perfect partner for delicate fennel in this light, yet creamy, soup. Serve with wafer-thin slices of toasted sourdough bread.

2 tbsp. olive oil, plus extra for brushing
1 onion, chopped
2 fennel bulbs
3 1/4 cups vegetable stock

1/2 cup vermouth
1/4 cup heavy cream
Salt and ground black pepper

Heat the oil in a large saucepan. Add the onion and cook gently for about 4 minutes. Trim any leaves from the fennel and reserve them for garnish, and then chop the bulbs. Add the fennel and stock to the pan, and bring to a boil. Reduce the heat, cover, and simmer for about 15 minutes, until the fennel is tender.

Process the soup in a food processor or blender until smooth. Return it to the pan and pour in the vermouth. Stir in the cream, add salt and pepper to taste, and warm the soup through without boiling.

Ladle the soup into bowls and sprinkle with the reserved fennel leaves, then serve immediately, while piping hot.

Serves 4

asparagus soup with smoked salmon crostini

see variations page 222

Light, creamy, and delicate with the distinctive taste of asparagus, this simple soup has elegant crostini floating on top to make a stunning first course for any special meal.

2 1/2 bunches asparagus
3 tbsp. butter
1 onion, finely chopped
1 1/2 tbsp. all-purpose flour
4 1/4 cups vegetable stock
5 tbsp. heavy cream

Juice of about 1/4 lemon, to taste
Salt and ground black pepper
4 slices small baguette, toasted until golden
2 tbsp. mayonnaise
1 slice smoked salmon, cut into 4 strips

Cut off and reserve the asparagus tips, then slice the stems. Melt the butter in a large saucepan. Add the onion and cook for 4 minutes. Stir in the flour and cook for 1 minute, then gradually stir in the stock. Add the asparagus stems and bring to a boil. Reduce the heat, cover, and simmer for about 10 minutes, until the asparagus is tender.

Meanwhile, cook the asparagus tips in boiling water for 2 to 6 minutes, until tender. Drain and refresh under cold water. Process the soup in a food processor or blender until smooth, then return it to the pan. Stir in the cream, lemon juice, and salt and pepper to taste, and all but 4 of the asparagus tips. Heat without boiling. Ladle the soup into bowls. Top the toasts with mayonnaise, smoked salmon, and asparagus tips. Float the crostini in the soups.

Serves 4

rich porcini soup with sherry & nutmeg

see variations page 223

Porcini mushrooms have a wonderfully rich, smoky flavor. This soup uses dried mushrooms, so you can enjoy it all year round, not only when porcini are in season.

1 oz. dried porcini
1 cup boiling water
3 tbsp. butter
1 onion, chopped
3 garlic cloves, crushed
1 tbsp. all-purpose flour
5 cups vegetable stock

1 lb. cremini mushrooms, sliced
1/2 cup sherry
1/2 cup heavy cream
1 tsp. freshly grated nutmeg
Salt and ground black pepper
Chopped fresh parsley, to garnish

Soak the porcini in the boiling water for 20 minutes. Melt the butter in a large saucepan. Add the onion and garlic, and cook gently for 4 minutes. Stir in the flour and cook for 1 minute, then gradually stir in the stock. Add the cremini mushrooms, porcini, and their soaking water. Bring to a boil, reduce the heat, cover, and simmer for 20 minutes.

Remove a ladleful of the mushrooms from the pan, then pour the rest of the soup into a food processor or blender. Process until smooth, then return the soup to the pan, and stir in the sherry, cream, nutmeg, and reserved mushrooms. Add salt and pepper to taste and warm through without boiling. Serve garnished with parsley.

Serves 4

sweet bell pepper & salmon soup with fresh basil

see variations page 224

Fresh and tangy with the taste of peppers and orange, this stunning bright orange-red soup, flecked with green basil, makes a fabulous appetizer for a special dinner.

2 tbsp. olive oil
1 onion, chopped
2 garlic cloves, crushed
3 red bell peppers, seeded and chopped
3 yellow bell peppers, seeded and chopped
2 tsp. ground coriander

5 cups vegetable stock
Juice of 2 oranges
Two 5 oz. salmon fillets, skinned
Handful of fresh basil leaves, torn, plus extra,
    to garnish
Salt and ground black pepper

Heat the olive oil in a large saucepan. Add the onion and garlic, and cook for 4 minutes. Add the peppers and sauté gently for 5 minutes. Stir in the coriander, then add the stock and orange juice, and bring to a boil. Reduce the heat, cover, and simmer for about 20 minutes.

Meanwhile, poach the salmon in a shallow pan of barely simmering water for about 8 minutes, until just cooked. Use a spatula to transfer the fish to a plate and let cool until cool enough to handle. Flake the fish into large pieces and set aside.

Process the soup into a food processor or blender until smooth. Add the basil and salmon, with salt and pepper to taste. Ladle the soup into bowls and serve sprinkled with fresh basil.

Serves 4

classic beef consommé

see variations page 225

This old-fashioned appetizer still makes a truly sophisticated opening to a meal. The crystal-clear broth has a wonderfully rich flavor — perfect for whetting the appetite.

7 1/2 cups beef stock
2 shallots, chopped
2 leeks, sliced
2 celery stalks, sliced
2 carrots, chopped
8–12 oz. lean ground beef

2 egg whites
2 egg shells, crushed
2 tbsp. sherry
Salt and ground black pepper
Finely shredded celery, to garnish (optional)

Bring the stock to a boil in a large saucepan. In a separate large saucepan, mix the shallots, leeks, celery, carrots, beef, egg whites, and egg shells. Whisk in the stock, then bring to a boil, whisking all the time. Reduce the heat and simmer gently for 1 hour.

Scoop off the thick layer of scum from the surface of the broth. Scald a metal sieve, piece of cheesecloth, and clean saucepan or large bowl with boiling water. Line the sieve with the cheesecloth and place it over the pan or bowl. Strain the stock through this sieve.

Stir in the sherry with salt and pepper to taste, then heat through and serve. Garnish with fine shreds of celery, if desired.

Serves 4

spiced cherry tomato & vodka soup with seared scallops

see base recipe page 199

spiced cherry tomato & vodka soup with garlic scallops
Prepare the basic recipe, adding 1 crushed garlic clove to the marinade for the scallops.

spiced cherry tomato & vodka soup with seared squid
Prepare the basic recipe, using 6 cleaned squid in place of the scallops. Pull the tentacles from the body, then slice the body into rings, and continue as before, searing for about 1 minute until just cooked.

spiced cherry tomato & vodka soup
Prepare the basic recipe, omitting the scallops.

spiced cherry tomato & vodka soup with shrimp
Prepare the basic recipe, using 12 shelled, deveined raw tiger shrimp in place of the scallops.

iced cherry tomato & vodka soup
Prepare the basic recipe, omitting the scallops. Leave the soup to cool, then chill it for at least 2 hours before serving.

variations

garden pea soup with prosciutto croûtes

see base recipe page 201

garden pea soup with asparagus croûtes
Prepare the basic recipe, using 4 cooked asparagus spears in place of
the prosciutto.

garden pea soup with asparagus & prosciutto croûtes
Prepare the basic recipe, adding a lightly cooked asparagus spear to each
prosciutto croûte.

garden pea soup with smoked salmon croûtes
Prepare the basic recipe, topping each croûte with a strip of smoked salmon
in place of the prosciutto.

garden pea soup with anchovy & egg croûtes
Prepare the basic recipe, omitting the prosciutto and mustard. Hard-cook
2 small eggs, then drain, cool, and shell. Cut the eggs into fourths. Top each
croûte with a drained anchovy and a piece of egg.

garden pea soup with artichoke croûtes
Prepare the basic recipe, using 4 marinated artichoke hearts in place
of the prosciutto.

variations

spicy crab & coconut soup

see base recipe page 202

spicy crab & coconut soup with noodles
Prepare the basic recipe. Cook 4 oz. egg noodles according to the instructions on the package, drain, and divide among four bowls. Ladle in the soup.

spicy crab & coconut soup with rice
Prepare the basic recipe and serve the soup ladled over cooked rice.

spicy shrimp & coconut soup
Prepare the basic recipe, using 24 peeled cooked tiger shrimp in place of the crabmeat.

spicy salmon & coconut soup
Prepare the basic recipe, adding 2 skinned, boneless salmon fillets (5 oz.), cut into strips, in place of the crabmeat. Cook for about 2 minutes longer, until the salmon is cooked through.

fava bean & sugar snap soup

see base recipe page 204

fava bean & sugar snap soup with parmesan cheese
Prepare the basic recipe, sprinkling Parmesan cheese shavings over
each serving.

fava bean & sugar snap soup with spinach
Prepare the basic recipe, adding 2 large handfuls of baby spinach
(or shredded large leaves) just before the end of the cooking time.

fava bean & sugar snap soup with bacon
Prepare the basic recipe, frying 3 roughly chopped bacon slices with
the shallots and garlic.

fava bean & sugar snap soup with spicy chorizo
Prepare the basic recipe, frying 2 oz. diced chorizo with the shallots
and garlic.

fava bean & sugar snap soup with mint
Prepare the basic recipe, using 1 tablespoon chopped fresh mint in place
of the basil.

variations

creamed artichoke soup with anchovy toasts

see base recipe page 205

creamed artichoke soup with lemon, with anchovy toasts
Prepare the basic recipe, stirring 1/2 teaspoon grated lemon zest into the
soup with the mint.

creamed artichoke soup and roasted pepper soup
Prepare the basic recipe, adding 2 bottled roasted peppers to the pan just
before blending.

creamed artichoke soup with garlic toasts
Prepare the basic recipe, omitting the anchovies and butter. Instead, rub
the toasts with a cut clove of garlic and drizzle with a little olive oil.

creamed artichoke soup with chives & anchovy toasts
Prepare the basic recipe, using 2 tablespoons snipped fresh chives in place
of the mint.

variations

vermouth & fennel soup

see base recipe page 207

white wine & fennel soup
Prepare the basic recipe, using white wine in place of the vermouth.

vermouth & fennel soup with chives
Prepare the basic recipe, stirring 2 tablespoons snipped fresh chives into the finished soup.

vermouth & celery soup
Prepare the basic recipe, using 8 celery sticks in place of the fennel.

vermouth & fennel soup with rosemary
Prepare the basic recipe, adding a sprig of rosemary to the stock. Simmer, then remove the rosemary before blending.

variations

asparagus soup with smoked salmon crostini

see base recipe page 208

simple cream of asparagus soup
Prepare the basic recipe, omitting the smoked salmon crostini.

asparagus soup with salami crostini
Prepare the basic recipe, topping each crostini with a twist of salami in place of the smoked salmon.

asparagus soup with caviar crostini
Prepare the basic recipe, using sour cream in place of the mayonnaise, and a dollop of caviar in place of each smoked salmon strip.

asparagus soup with smoked trout crostini
Prepare the basic recipe, topping each crostini with a large flake of smoked trout in place of the strip of smoked salmon.

rich porcini soup with sherry & nutmeg

see base recipe page 211

fresh porcini soup
Prepare the basic recipe, omitting the dried porcini, and using a mixture
of fresh porcini mushrooms and cremini mushrooms (1 lb. total weight). The
additional fresh mushrooms will give up their moisture instead of the
soaking liquid from the dried porcini.

porcini soup with white wine
Prepare the basic recipe, using white wine in place of the sherry.

porcini soup with goat cheese croûtes
Prepare the basic recipe. To serve, toast 4 slices of baguette until golden
on both sides, then top with goat cheese, and float on each bowl of soup.

porcini soup with walnut & blue cheese toasts
Prepare the basic recipe. To serve, toast 4 slices of walnut bread until golden
on one side. Turn over, top with a sliver of blue cheese, and broil until
melting, then serve with the soup.

porcini soup with thyme
Prepare the basic recipe, adding 1 teaspoon fresh thyme leaves with the
stock. Omit the parsley.

variations

sweet bell pepper & salmon soup with fresh basil

see base recipe page 212

sweet bell pepper & jumbo shrimp soup

Prepare the basic recipe, using 8–12 oz. peeled cooked jumbo shrimp in place of the salmon. Add to the soup about 1 minute before serving to warm through.

chilled sweet bell pepper soup with fresh basil

Prepare the basic recipe, omitting the salmon. Leave to cool, then chill for at least 2 hours before serving.

sweet bell pepper & salmon soup with fresh chives

Prepare the basic recipe, using 3 tablespoons snipped fresh chives in place of the basil.

sweet bell pepper & salmon soup with fresh mint

Prepare the basic recipe, using 1 handful of fresh mint leaves in place of the basil.

sweet bell pepper soup with fresh basil

Prepare the basic recipe, omitting the salmon.

variations

classic beef consommé

see base recipe page 215

chicken consommé
Prepare the basic recipe, using chicken stock in place of the beef stock,
and ground chicken in place of the beef.

chili beef consommé
Prepare the basic recipe, adding 2 seeded, chopped red chilies with the
other vegetables.

rich beef consommé with port
Prepare the basic recipe, using port in place of the sherry.

beef consommé with scallions
Prepare the basic recipe, adding 4 finely sliced scallions to the consommé
just before ladling into bowls.

asian flavors

Light broths with noodles, rich and creamy coconut milk soups, and concoctions spiked with fragrant herbs and spices are all classic Asian combinations. Try your hand at making any one of these soups and bring exotic flavors to your table.

malaysian shrimp laksa

see variations page 244

A chunky seafood broth ladled over freshly cooked noodles, this tasty soup makes a superlative meal in a bowl.

2 shallots, chopped
3 red chilies, seeded and chopped
1 garlic clove
2 tsp. grated fresh ginger
Grated zest of 1 lime
1 tsp. ground turmeric
1 tsp. ground coriander
2 tbsp. Thai fish sauce
2 tbsp. peanuts

2 tbsp. sunflower oil
4 1/4 cups fish or vegetable stock
8 oz. wheat noodles
Scant 1 cup coconut cream
1 tsp. brown sugar
12 oz. raw tiger shrimp, shelled
    and deveined
4 handfuls beansprouts
Large handful of fresh cilantro leaves

Process the shallots, chilies, garlic, ginger, lime zest, turmeric, coriander, fish sauce, and peanuts to a paste in a food processor. Heat the oil in a large saucepan and sauté the paste for 2 minutes. Stir in the stock. Bring to a boil, reduce the heat, and simmer for 10 minutes.

Cook the noodles according to the package instructions. Drain and divide among 4 bowls. Stir the coconut cream and sugar into the broth, add the shrimp, and simmer for about 2 minutes, until the shrimp are pink and cooked. Remove from the heat, stir in the beansprouts and half the cilantro. Ladle the broth over the noodles, top with more cilantro leaves and serve.

Serves 4

thai-style coconut chicken noodle soup

see variations page 245

This hot, spicy coconut broth ladled over fine wheat noodles makes a delicious, sustaining meal. Try it as a spicy alternative to traditional chicken noodle soup.

2 tbsp. sunflower oil
3 shallots, finely chopped
4 fresh green chilies, seeded and chopped
2 tsp. grated fresh ginger
2 garlic cloves, crushed
2 lemongrass stalks, chopped
4 kaffir lime leaves, shredded
1 3/4 cups coconut milk
3 1/2 cups chicken stock

2 skinless boneless chicken breasts, cut into
    small bite-size pieces
6 baby corn, quartered lengthwise
8 oz. fine wheat noodles
1 to 2 tbsp. Thai fish sauce
Juice of about 1 lime, to taste
Bunch of scallions, sliced
Handful of fresh cilantro

Heat the oil in a saucepan. Add the shallots, chilies, ginger, and garlic. Cook for 3 minutes. Stir in the lemongrass, lime leaves, coconut milk, and stock. Boil, then reduce the heat, add the chicken, and simmer gently for 10 minutes. Add the corn and cook for 2 to 3 minutes.

Meanwhile, cook the noodles according to the package instructions, drain, and divide among four bowls. Add fish sauce and lime juice to taste to the soup. Stir in the scallions and half the cilantro. Ladle the soup over the noodles and sprinkle with the remaining cilantro.

Serves 4

miso broth with ramen & seared tuna

see variations page 246

This light Japanese broth is poured over tender ramen noodles (fine, quick-cooking wheat noodles) and topped with seared tuna to make a healthy and delicious meal.

4 1/4 cups water
4 tbsp. miso paste
9 oz. ramen noodles
4 tuna steaks (each about 4 oz.)

Salt and ground black pepper
Groundnut or sunflower oil, for greasing
4 scallions, sliced

Heat the water and miso paste gently in a large saucepan, stirring until the miso has dissolved. Bring to a boil, then reduce the heat, cover, and simmer gently while preparing the remaining ingredients.

Cook the noodles according to the package instructions, drain, and divide among four bowls. Season the tuna steaks with salt and ground black pepper. Brush a nonstick skillet with oil and heat until hot. Sear the tuna for about 2 minutes on each side until cooked, but still pink in the middle. Place a tuna steak in each bowl and scatter with scallions.

Ladle the broth into the bowls and serve immediately.

Serves 4

red curry soup with duck

see variations page 247

The distinctive, meaty flavor and firm texture of duck makes a good base for the flavors of a classic Thai red curry in this wholesome soup.

2 tbsp. sunflower oil
2 shallots, finely chopped
2 red chilies, seeded and chopped
2 tsp. grated fresh ginger
2 tsp. Thai red curry paste
5 cups chicken stock
2 skinless boneless duck breasts, cut into
  bite-size strips

1/2 cup coconut cream
1 tsp. brown sugar
Juice of about 1 lime, to taste
1 tbsp. Thai fish sauce
1 green bell pepper, seeded and sliced
1 red bell pepper, seeded and sliced
4 baby corn, quartered
Handful of basil leaves, to serve

Heat the oil in a large saucepan. Add the shallots, chilies, and ginger, and cook for 2 minutes. Stir in the curry paste and sauté for another 2 minutes. Add the stock and duck, and bring to a boil. Reduce the heat, cover, and simmer for about 15 minutes.

Stir in the coconut cream, sugar, lime juice, and fish sauce to taste. Add the vegetables and simmer for 2 minutes, until just tender but retaining a crisp bite.

Ladle the soup into bowls, scatter with the basil leaves and serve.

Serves 4

vietnamese beef noodle soup

see variations page 248

Based on the classic soup served by Vietnamese street vendors, this broth is refreshing, yet substantial. The wafer-thin slices of beef are cooked very lightly in the hot stock.

5 cups good-quality fresh beef stock
2 tsp. grated fresh ginger
4 cloves
1 cinnamon stick
4 star anise
1 tsp. black peppercorns
1 tbsp. fish sauce

7 oz. flat rice noodles
9 oz. beef sirloin, cut into wafer-thin slices
2 red chilies, seeded and finely sliced
Bunch of scallions, sliced
2 handfuls beansprouts
Large handful of fresh cilantro leaves
1 lime, quartered

Put the stock in a large saucepan. Add the ginger, cloves, cinnamon, star anise, peppercorns, and fish sauce, and bring to a boil. Reduce the heat, cover, and simmer for about 1 hour.

Strain the stock into a clean pan and heat until simmering. Put the noodles in a bowl, pour boiling water over them, and leave to stand for 5 minutes until tender, then drain, and divide among four bowls.

Add the beef to the noodles in the serving bowls. Sprinkle with the chilies, scallions, and beansprouts. Ladle over the hot stock and sprinkle with the cilantro. Serve with the lime wedges for squeezing over juice to taste.

Serves 4

hot-and-sour crab soup

see variations page 249

Fresh and fiery, this deliciously fragrant soup makes a lively light lunch or appetizer. If you prefer milder flavors, simply use fewer chilies.

2 shallots, finely chopped
2 garlic cloves, crushed
2 tsp. grated fresh ginger
3 red bird's eye chilies, seeded and finely chopped, plus 1 seeded, and shredded
1 tbsp. sweet chili sauce
4 kaffir lime leaves, shredded
5 cups fish or vegetable stock

2 tsp. brown sugar
Juice of 1 lime
1 tsp. Thai fish sauce
Two 6-oz. cans white crabmeat
4 handfuls beansprouts
5 scallions, sliced
Handful of fresh cilantro leaves

Put the shallots, garlic, ginger, chopped chilies, chili sauce, lime leaves, and stock in a large saucepan. Bring to a boil, then reduce the heat, cover, and simmer for about 20 minutes.

Strain the stock into a clean pan and stir in the sugar, lime juice, and fish sauce. Divide the crabmeat among four bowls. Top each portion with a handful of beansprouts and sprinkle with the scallions and shredded chili. Ladle over the stock, sprinkle with cilantro leaves, and serve immediately.

Serves 4

fiery thai broth with tofu & scallions

see variations page 250

Hot, light, and fragrant; laden with tender green cabbage and healthy tofu, this full-flavored broth makes a delicious start to an Asian-style meal.

2 tbsp. sunflower oil
3 green bird's eye chilies, seeded and chopped
2 tsp. Thai green curry paste
5 cups vegetable stock
4 kaffir lime leaves, shredded
2 tsp. brown sugar

Juice of about 1 lime, to taste
1/4 small green cabbage, shredded
5 oz. deep-fried tofu, cubed
Bunch of scallions, sliced
Handful of fresh cilantro leaves

Heat the oil in a large saucepan. Add the chilies and curry paste, and fry for about 30 seconds. Pour in the stock and add the lime leaves, then bring to a boil. Reduce the heat, cover, and simmer for about 20 minutes.

Strain the broth into a clean pan and stir in the sugar and lime juice to taste. Add the cabbage and simmer for about 1 minute, then add the tofu and cook for 30 to 60 seconds, until the cabbage is just tender.

Ladle the soup into bowls, garnish with scallions and cilantro, and serve.

Serves 4

chinese-style broth with wontons

see variations page 251

This simple, fragrant broth, highlighted with the smoky flavor of sesame, makes a delicious light meal or appetizer.

for the wontons

1 tbsp. sunflower oil
1 tsp. sesame oil
1/2 small onion, grated
5 drained canned water chestnuts, finely chopped
2 oz. ground pork
1 tsp. soy sauce
Ground black pepper
16 wonton wrappers

for the broth

5 cups vegetable stock
3 tbsp. mirin or sherry
1 tsp. brown sugar
2 tsp. soy sauce
1 tsp. sesame oil
4 scallions, sliced

For the wontons, heat the oils in a small nonstick skillet. Sauté the onion, chestnuts, and pork for 3 minutes, until the pork is cooked. Mix in the soy sauce and black pepper. Lay a wonton wrapper on a board and dampen the edges. Put a teaspoonful of filling in the center, gather up the wrapper, and twist it to seal the filling in a little purse. Repeat with the remaining ingredients. Cook the wontons in a steamer for 12 minutes, until tender.

Meanwhile, bring the stock to a boil in a large saucepan. Reduce the heat and stir in the mirin or sherry, sugar, soy sauce, and sesame oil. Put four wontons in each bowl, ladle the hot soup over, scatter with scallions, and serve.

Serves 4

hot szechuan-style noodle soup with cilantro omelet

see variations page 252

This hot and spicy, colorful broth is ladled over rice noodles and topped with strips of fragrant omelet. It makes a delicious light meal or appetizer.

4 oz. fine rice noodles
5 cups chicken or vegetable stock
2 tsp. grated fresh ginger
1 red bird's eye chili, seeded and
    finely chopped
1 tsp. freshly ground black pepper
1 tbsp. tomato paste

1 tbsp. soy sauce
1 tbsp. rice vinegar
1 egg
Handful of fresh cilantro, chopped
1 tbsp. sunflower oil
1/2 cup canned sliced bamboo shoots, drained
5 scallions, sliced

Soak the noodles in a bowl of boiling water for 5 minutes. Drain and snip into 2 1/2-in lengths, then set aside. Bring the stock, ginger, chili, black pepper, tomato paste, soy sauce, and vinegar to a boil in a large saucepan. Reduce the heat and simmer for 5 minutes.

Meanwhile, beat the egg and stir in the cilantro. Heat the oil in a small skillet, add the egg, and swirl it around the skillet to form a thin layer. Cook for 2 minutes, until set. Slide the omelet onto a board. Roll up and thinly slice the omelet, then shake out into strips. Add the noodles and bamboo shoots to the soup, and heat for 1 minute. Ladle the soup into bowls, sprinkle with scallions, and top with omelet strips, then serve at once.

Serves 4

vietnamese-style sour fish soup

see variations page 253

Hot and spicy, with succulent fish, juicy pineapple, and crisp beansprouts, this soup is delicious at any time of day.

2 tbsp. vegetable oil
2 shallots, finely chopped
2 garlic cloves, crushed
2 tsp. grated fresh ginger
2 hot red chilies, seeded and chopped
2 lemongrass stalks, chopped
5 cups vegetable stock
2 tsp. tamarind paste
1 tbsp. brown sugar

1 tsp. fish sauce
4 tomatoes, peeled and chopped
1 cup fresh pineapple, peeled, cored, and cut
　　into bite-size pieces
1 lb. firm white fish, skinned and cut into
　　bite-size pieces
2 handfuls beansprouts
Handful of fresh cilantro leaves

Heat the oil in a large saucepan. Add the shallots, garlic, ginger, and chilies, and cook for about 2 minutes. Add the lemongrass and stock, and bring to a boil. Reduce the heat, cover, and simmer for about 30 minutes.

Strain the stock into a clean pan and stir in the tamarind paste, sugar, and fish sauce. Add the tomatoes and pineapple, and simmer for about 3 minutes. Add the fish and simmer for 2 to 3 minutes longer, until cooked through.

Ladle the soup into bowls. Top with beansprouts and cilantro, and serve immediately.

Serves 4

variations

malaysian shrimp laksa

see base recipe page 227

malaysian salmon laksa
Prepare the basic recipe, using 3 skinned, cubed 5 oz. salmon fillets in place of the shrimp.

malaysian shrimp laksa with rice noodles
Prepare the basic recipe, using flat rice noodles in place of wheat noodles.

malaysian shrimp laksa with scallions
Prepare the basic recipe, adding 1 bunch of sliced scallions with the beansprouts.

vegetarian laksa
Prepare the basic recipe omitting the fish sauce and shrimp, and seasoning with salt. Add 10 oz. cubed tofu and warm through for 1 minute before adding the beansprouts and cilantro.

malaysian chicken laksa
Prepare the basic recipe, adding 2 skinless, boneless chicken breasts, sliced into small bite-size pieces, with the stock and coconut milk.

variations

thai-style coconut chicken noodle soup

see base recipe page 229

thai-style coconut shrimp noodle soup
Prepare the basic recipe, omitting the chicken. Add 24 shelled, deveined raw tiger shrimp 2 minutes before the end of cooking and simmer until pink and cooked through.

thai-style coconut tofu noodle soup
Prepare the basic recipe, omitting the chicken. Add 10 oz. deep-fried tofu cubes with the scallions.

thai-style coconut crab noodle soup
Prepare the basic recipe, omitting the chicken. Add two 6-oz. cans white crabmeat with the scallions.

thai-style coconut vegetable noodle soup
Prepare the basic recipe, omitting the chicken. Add 1 seeded, sliced red bell pepper, a large handful of halved button mushrooms, and large handful broccoli florets with the corn.

thai-style coconut fish soup
Prepare the basic recipe, omitting the chicken. Add 10 1/2 oz. cubed, skinned, firm white fish 2 to 3 minutes before the end of cooking.

miso broth with ramen & seared tuna

see base recipe page 230

miso broth with ramen & tofu
Prepare the basic recipe, omitting the tuna. Add 9 oz. cubed silken tofu to the broth and warm through for 1 minute, then ladle into bowls, and sprinkle with the scallions.

miso broth with ramen & seared salmon
Prepare the basic recipe, using skinned salmon fillets in place of the tuna steaks. Sear on each side for about 4 minutes, until cooked, then finish as in the basic recipe.

miso broth with ramen & jumbo shrimp
Prepare the basic recipe, omitting the tuna steaks. Add 12 oz. shelled, deveined raw jumbo shrimp to the broth 2 minutes before serving. Cook until pink and cooked through, then ladle over the noodles.

miso broth with ramen & charbroiled chicken
Slice 3 skinless, boneless chicken breasts into strips. Combine 2 crushed garlic cloves, 1 tablespoon sunflower oil, and salt and pepper. Toss with the chicken and marinate for 1 hour. Prepare the basic recipe, omitting the tuna. Heat a ridged griddle pan, then cook the chicken for about 2 minutes on each side. Scatter over the cooked noodles and ladle the broth on top.

variations

red curry soup with duck

see base recipe page 232

red curry soup with duck & steamed rice
Prepare the basic recipe. To serve, place a couple of heaped spoonfuls of cooked Jasmine rice in the bottom of each bowl before ladling in the soup.

red curry soup with chicken
Prepare the basic recipe, using 2 skinless, boneless chicken breasts in place of the duck.

red curry soup with shrimp
Prepare the basic recipe, omitting the duck. Add 12 oz. peeled, deveined raw tiger shrimp with the vegetables and cook until they are pink and cooked.

red curry soup with tofu
Prepare the basic recipe, omitting the duck. Add 9 oz. deep-fried tofu cubes with the vegetables.

variations

vietnamese beef noodle soup

see base recipe page 233

vietnamese chicken noodle soup
Prepare the basic recipe, using chicken stock in place of the beef stock, and 2 sliced, skinless cooked chicken breasts in place of the beef.

vietnamese pork noodle soup
Prepare the basic recipe, using chicken stock in place of the beef stock, and 2 sliced, cooked 5 oz. pork loin steaks in place of the beef.

vietnamese shrimp noodle soup
Prepare the basic recipe, using fish or vegetable stock in place of the beef stock, and 20 cooked, peeled tiger shrimp in place of the beef.

vietnamese crab noodle soup
Prepare the basic recipe, using fish or vegetable stock in place of the beef stock, and using two 6-oz. cans white crabmeat in place of the beef.

variations

hot-and-sour crab soup

see base recipe page 235

hot-and-sour crab soup with noodles
Prepare the basic recipe. Toward the end of cooking time, soak 4 oz. rice noodles in boiling water for 5 minutes, then drain, and divide among the four bowls. Continue as in the basic recipe.

hot-and-sour chicken soup
Prepare the basic recipe, using 2 sliced, skinless cooked chicken breasts in place of the crabmeat.

hot-and-sour shrimp soup
Prepare the basic recipe, using 20 peeled cooked tiger shrimp in place of the crabmeat.

hot-and-sour tofu soup
Prepare the basic recipe, using 9 oz. cubed silken tofu in place of the crabmeat.

hot-and-sour shiitake mushroom soup
Prepare the basic recipe, adding 6 quartered fresh shiitake mushrooms to the strained stock and simmering for 4 minutes. Continue as in the basic recipe, omitting the crabmeat.

variations

fiery thai broth with tofu & scallions

see base recipe page 236

fiery thai broth with tofu & vegetables
Prepare the basic recipe, adding 1 large carrot, cut into thin batons, with the tofu. Put a handful of baby spinach in each bowl before pouring in the soup.

fiery thai broth with tofu, cauliflower & scallions
Prepare the basic recipe, adding large handful bite-size cauliflower florets in place of the cabbage.

fiery thai broth with tofu, broccoli & scallions
Prepare the basic recipe, adding large handful bite-size broccoli florets in place of the cabbage.

fiery thai broth with smoked mackerel & scallions
Skin 2 (approx. 6 oz.) smoked mackerel fillets and break the flesh into large flakes, discarding bones. Prepare the basic recipe, adding the smoked mackerel in place of the tofu.

fiery thai broth with tofu, scallions & jasmine rice
Prepare the basic recipe, spooning 2 tablespoons cooked Jasmine rice into each bowl before ladling in the soup.

variations

chinese-style broth with wontons

see base recipe page 239

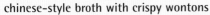

chinese-style broth with crispy wontons
Prepare the basic recipe. Instead of steaming the wontons, deep-fry them for about 4 minutes, until golden, in oil heated to 375°F (190°C). Drain on paper towels before putting in the bowls.

chinese-style broth with tofu
Prepare the basic recipe, omitting the wontons. Add 9 oz. tofu to the stock and warm through just before serving.

chinese-style broth with carrots & scallions
Prepare the basic recipe, omitting the wontons and simmering 1 large carrot, cut into thin batons, in the soup for 2 minutes before serving.

chinese-style broth with chicken wontons
Prepare the basic recipe, using ground chicken in place of the pork.

chinese style broth with cabbage
Prepare the basic recipe, adding 1/4 small shredded cabbage to the broth 1 to 2 minutes before serving. Simmer until just tender.

variations

hot szechuan-style noodle soup with cilantro omelet

see base recipe page 240

hot szechuan-style chicken noodle soup with cilantro omelet
Prepare the basic recipe, adding 2 shredded, cooked, skinless chicken breasts with the noodles and bamboo shoots.

hot szechuan-style noodle soup with tofu & cilantro omelet
Prepare the basic recipe, adding 9 oz. cubed silken tofu with the noodles and bamboo shoots.

hot szechuan-style noodle soup with cabbage & cilantro omelet
Prepare the basic recipe, adding 1/4 small shredded cabbage to the stock and simmering for 3 minutes before adding the noodles and bamboo shoots.

hot szechuan-style noodle soup with red bell pepper & cilantro omelet
Prepare the basic recipe, adding 1 seeded red bell pepper, cut into fine strips, with the noodles and bamboo shoots.

variations

vietnamese-style sour fish soup

see base recipe page 243

vietnamese-style sour shrimp soup
Prepare the basic recipe, using 28 peeled raw tiger shrimp in place of
the fish.

vietnamese-style sour fish soup with bamboo shoots
Prepare the basic recipe, adding 1/2 cup sliced bamboo shoots with the fish.

vietnamese-style sour tofu soup
Prepare the basic recipe, adding 9 oz. cubed silken tofu in place of the fish.
Simmer for 1 minute, then serve.

vietnamese-style sour chicken soup
Prepare the basic recipe, adding 3 cooked, skinless chicken breasts, cut into
bite-size pieces, in place of the fish.

vietnamese-style sour fish soup with mango
Prepare the basic recipe, using 2 small peeled, pitted mangoes, cut into bite-
size chunks, in place of the pineapple.

fruity flavors

Most people think of vegetables, meat, poultry, and seafood when they think of soup, but soups made with fruits are wonderful too, whether it's a simple soup flavored with orange or a sweet, fruity soup you could serve for dessert.

spiced chicken & apricot soup

see variations page 274

Tangy and light, yet fragrant and fruity with cinnamon and apricot, this soup makes a lively alternative to plain chicken noodle soup when you need a little comfort.

2 tbsp. olive oil
1 onion, finely chopped
3 garlic cloves, crushed
2 skinless, boneless chicken breasts,
    cut into bite-size strips
5 cups chicken stock

2 tsp. ground cinnamon
1 tsp. ground ginger
1 cup ready-to-eat dried apricots, chopped
Salt and ground black pepper
2 tbsp. chopped fresh parsley

Heat the oil in a large saucepan. Add the onion and garlic, and cook gently for 4 minutes. Add the chicken, then pour in the stock, and stir in the cinnamon, ginger, and apricots.

Bring the soup to a boil. Reduce the heat, cover the pan, and simmer the soup for 20 minutes, until the chicken is cooked.

Add salt and pepper to taste. Sprinkle in the parsley and ladle the soup into bowls to serve.

Serves 4

cock-a-leekie with tender prunes

see variations page 275

This classic Scottish soup is a real meal in a bowl. Adding barley ensures it's sufficiently sustaining to ward off hunger pangs between meals.

1/2 cup (3 1/2 oz.) pearled barley
5 cups chicken stock
1 tsp. dried thyme
5 juniper berries, crushed
3 large leeks, trimmed and sliced

1 cup ready-to-eat dried prunes, cut into
   bite-size pieces
2 cooked chicken breasts, cut into bite-size
   pieces
Ground black pepper

Put the barley, stock, thyme, and juniper berries in a large saucepan. Bring to a boil, stir well, then reduce the heat, and cover the pan. Simmer the soup for about 25 minutes, until the barley is tender.

Add the leeks, prunes, and chicken to the soup. Re-cover and simmer for about 10 minutes, until the leeks are tender. Season with black pepper and ladle the soup into bowls.

Serves 4

hungarian cherry soup

see variations page 276

This sweet-sour cherry soup is rich and creamy, and traditionally served in small portions as an elegant appetizer. Instead of bowls, try serving the soup in stylish cups on saucers.

2 lb. morello (sour) cherries, pitted
2/3 cup superfine sugar
2 cinnamon sticks
1 3/4 cups red wine

1 3/4 cups water
1/2 cup light cream
Lemon juice, to taste
Crème fraîche, to serve

Put the cherries in a large saucepan and sprinkle with the sugar. Tuck in the cinnamon sticks and pour in the wine and water. Bring to a boil, then reduce the heat, cover, and simmer for about 20 minutes.

Remove the cinnamon sticks. Stir in the light cream, then check the flavor, adding a squeeze of lemon juice to taste. Ladle the soup into small bowls and serve topped with crème fraîche.

Serves 4

chilled melon soup

see variations page 277

Choose ripe, fragrant melons for this simple, refreshing summer appetizer — the more fabulous the flavor of the melons, the better the soup.

3 cantaloupe
Juice of 3 oranges

Juice of 1/2 to 1 lime, to taste
Fresh mint leaves, to garnish

Cut the melons in half and scoop out the seeds. Scoop the flesh into a food processor or blender. Add the orange juice and process until smooth.

Pour the soup into a large bowl and stir in lime juice to taste. Chill for at least 2 hours. Ladle the soup into bowls and serve garnished with fresh mint leaves.

Serves 4

greek egg & lemon soup

see variations page 278

This classic soup is known as avgolemono in Greece. It is sharp, creamy, packed with tiny rice-shaped pasta (orzo), and thickened with eggs.

5 cups vegetable or chicken stock
3–4 oz. orzo
3 eggs

Juice of 1 lemon
Salt and ground black pepper
Chopped fresh parsley, to garnish

Pour the stock into a large saucepan and bring to a boil. Add the orzo and cook for about 5 minutes, until tender. Remove the pan from the heat.

In a separate bowl, beat the eggs with the lemon juice and 1 tablespoon cold water, then gradually beat in a couple of ladlefuls of the hot stock. Stirring constantly, pour the egg mixture back into the saucepan of soup.

Add salt and pepper to taste and ladle the soup into bowls. Sprinkle with chopped fresh parsley and serve.

Serves 4

pear & blue cheese soup with prosciutto crisps

see variations page 279

Tangy blue cheese and sweet, tender pear may sound like an unlikely combination, but the result is sublime in this richly flavored soup. Serve it as an elegant appetizer.

2 tbsp. sunflower oil
1 onion, chopped
1 garlic clove, crushed
4 pears, peeled, cored, and chopped

3 1/4 cups vegetable stock
3 oz. blue cheese
Ground black pepper
4 strips prosciutto

Heat the oil in a large saucepan. Add the onion and garlic, and cook gently for 4 minutes. Add the pears and stock, and bring to a boil. Reduce the heat, cover the pan, and simmer for about 5 minutes, until the pears are tender.

Pour the soup into a food processor or blender, add the cheese, and process until smooth. Season to taste with pepper and keep warm.

Preheat the broiler. Lay the prosciutto on a rack in a broiler pan and broil until crisp. Snip the crisp strips into bite-size pieces. Ladle the soup into serving bowls, sprinkle with the prosciutto crisps, and serve immediately.

Serves 4

spicy chicken soup with chili & lime

see variations page 280

Unlike many fruit soups, which have a sweet flavor, the lime gives this soup a wonderfully sour, zesty twist that complements the aromatic spices and basil.

2 tbsp. sunflower oil
2 shallots, finely chopped
3 garlic cloves, crushed
1 tsp. grated fresh ginger
3 fresh green chilies, seeded and finely chopped

5 cups chicken stock
2 skinless cooked chicken breasts, cut into small bite-size pieces
Grated zest and juice of 1 lime
Handful of fresh basil leaves, torn

Heat the oil in a large saucepan. Add the shallots, garlic, ginger, and chilies, and cook for about 2 minutes. Pour in the stock and bring to a boil. Reduce the heat, cover the pan, and simmer for about 15 minutes.

Add the chicken to the soup and simmer for a further 1 to 2 minutes. Stir in the lime zest and juice. Ladle the soup into serving bowls, sprinkle with basil, and serve immediately.

Serves 4

strawberry and chili soup

see variations page 281

Served in small bowls, this fiery, refreshing soup makes a deliciously unusual appetizer.
It takes only minutes to prepare and is perfect for entertaining.

3 pints ripe strawberries, hulled
Juice of 3 oranges
1 1/2 fresh red chilies, seeded and chopped

Salt
Ice cubes, to serve (optional)
Fresh mint leaves, to garnish

Process the strawberries, orange juice, and chilies in a food processor or blender until
smooth. Add a pinch of salt and pulse to mix it in.

Pour the soup into small bowls, add a couple of ice cubes to each portion, if desired,
and serve garnished with mint.

Serves 4

fish & orange soup

see variations page 282

This light, fragrant citrus broth, with chunks of firm white fish, makes a stylish light meal, served with chunks of crusty bread.

2 tbsp. sunflower oil
1 onion, finely chopped
2 garlic cloves, crushed
5 cups fish stock
1/2 tsp. sweet paprika
1 tbsp. tomato paste

1 lb. firm white fish fillets, skinned
    and cubed
1 tsp. finely grated orange zest
Juice of 2 oranges
Salt and ground black pepper
Handful of chopped fresh parsley

Heat the oil in a large saucepan. Add the onion and garlic, and cook for about 4 minutes. Stir in the stock, paprika, and tomato paste, and simmer for about 5 minutes. Add the fish, orange zest, and juice, and simmer for 2 to 3 minutes, until the fish is just cooked.

Season the soup with salt and pepper to taste, then ladle it into serving bowls, and garnish with fresh parsley. Serve immediately.

Serves 4

duck & pomegranate soup

see variations page 283

Sweet, yet astringent, pomegranate and fruity, full-bodied port come together beautifully in this richly flavored soup.

2 boneless duck breasts
Salt and ground black pepper
2 shallots, finely chopped
2 garlic cloves, crushed
2 tbsp. all-purpose flour

4 1/4 cups chicken or duck stock
2 pomegranates
1/2 cup port
Handful of parsley, chopped

Score the duck skin in a lattice pattern and rub with salt. Heat a large nonstick saucepan. Add the duck, skin down, and cook for 10 minutes. Pour away most of the fat, leaving about 2 tablespoons in the pan, turn the duck, and cook for 4 to 5 minutes. Remove and set aside. Add the shallots and garlic. Cook gently for 2 to 3 minutes. Stir in the flour and cook for 1 minute. Gradually stir in the stock. Boil, reduce the heat, cover, and simmer for 10 minutes.

Meanwhile, halve the pomegranates. Hold one half over a bowl and tap the back of the peel with a wooden spoon to remove the seeds. Repeat with the remaining fruit. Reserve a quarter of the seeds. Put the remaining seeds in a sieve over a bowl, and press with a spoon to extract the juice. Stir the juice and port into the soup, with salt and pepper to taste.

Slice the duck into thin strips, add to the soup and warm through. Serve sprinkled with parsley and the reserved pomegranate seeds.

Serves 4

variations

spiced chicken & apricot soup

see base recipe page 255

spiced chicken & prune soup
Prepare the basic recipe, using ready-to-eat dried prunes in place of the apricots.

spiced chicken & apricot soup with couscous
Prepare the basic recipe. To serve, soak a generous 3/4 cup couscous in 3/4 cup boiling water for 5 minutes. Fluff up with a fork and add 1 tablespoon olive oil and a handful of chopped fresh parsley, then toss to combine. Spoon the couscous into each bowl of soup.

spiced chicken & apricot soup with honey
Prepare the basic recipe, stirring 2 teaspoons clear honey into the soup with the dried apricots.

spiced chicken soup with peppers & apricots
Prepare the basic recipe, adding 2 seeded, roughly chopped yellow bell peppers to the soup with the apricots.

spiced chicken noodle soup with apricots
Prepare the basic recipe, adding 4 oz. vermicelli to the soup about 3 minutes before the end of cooking time. Simmer until tender.

cock-a-leekie with tender prunes

see base recipe page 257

simple cock-a-leekie with tender prunes
Prepare the basic recipe, omitting the barley.

simple cock-a-leekie with rice
Prepare the basic recipe, omitting the barley. Put a couple of spoonfuls of cooked rice in each bowl and ladle the soup over it.

rich herb cock-a-leekie with tender prunes
Prepare the basic recipe, adding 1 bay leaf and 2 tablespoons chopped fresh parsley with the thyme. Sprinkle snipped fresh chives over the soup before serving.

vegetarian quorn cock-a-leekie with tender prunes
Prepare the basic recipe, using vegetable stock in place of chicken stock, and Quorn pieces in place of the chicken.

chunky bean cock-a-leekie with tender prunes
Prepare the basic recipe, adding a 14-oz. can drained and rinsed mixed beans with the leeks, prunes, and chicken.

variations

hungarian cherry soup

see base recipe page 258

chilled hungarian cherry soup
Prepare the basic recipe. Leave the soup to cool, then chill it for at least 3 hours before serving.

hungarian cherry soup with port
Prepare the basic recipe, using 1 1/4 cups red wine and 1/2 cup port instead of all red wine.

ginger-spiced cherry soup
Prepare the basic recipe, adding 1 1/2 teaspoons ground ginger with the cinnamon sticks.

cherry & vanilla soup
Prepare the basic recipe, adding 1 teaspoon natural vanilla extract with the light cream.

cherry & almond soup
Prepare the basic recipe, adding 1 teaspoon almond extract with the light cream, and sprinkling the finished soup with toasted slivered almonds.

chilled melon soup

see base recipe page 261

chilled watermelon soup
Prepare the basic recipe, using 4 1/2 lb. watermelon in place of the
cantaloupe.

chilled honeydew soup
Prepare the basic recipe, using 4 1/2 lb. honeydew melons in place
of the cantaloupe.

chilled melon & ginger soup
Prepare the basic recipe, adding 1 teaspoon grated fresh ginger to the
food processor or blender with the melon.

chilled melon soup with mango sorbet
Prepare the basic recipe, adding a scoop of mango sorbet to each bowl
of soup when serving.

variations

greek egg & lemon soup

see base recipe page 262

greek egg & lemon soup with chives
Prepare the basic recipe, sprinkling the finished soup with chives instead of parsley.

greek egg & lemon soup with cauliflower
Cut half a small cauliflower into bite-size florets. Prepare the basic recipe, adding the cauliflower with the orzo.

greek egg & lemon soup with spinach
Prepare the basic recipe, stirring 2 large handfuls of baby spinach into the stock before adding the egg mixture.

greek egg & lemon soup with chicken
Prepare the basic recipe, adding 8–12 oz. skinless cooked chicken, cut into small bite-size pieces, just before the end of cooking.

greek egg & lemon soup with lettuce
Prepare the basic recipe, adding 1 shredded Romaine lettuce to the stock about 1 minute before stirring in the egg mixture.

variations

pear & blue cheese soup with prosciutto crisps

see base recipe page 265

pear & goat cheese soup with prosciutto crisps
Prepare the basic recipe, using goat cheese in place of the blue cheese.

apple & blue cheese soup with prosciutto crisps
Prepare the basic recipe, using apples in place of the pears.

pear & blue cheese soup with prosciutto crisps & fresh mint
Prepare the basic recipe, sprinkling the soup with chopped fresh mint
before serving.

pear & blue cheese soup with garlic toasts
Prepare the basic recipe, omitting the prosciutto. To serve, toast 8 slices of
baguette until golden on both sides, then rub with a halved clove of garlic,
and drizzle with olive oil. Serve with the soup.

spicy chicken soup with chili & lime

see base recipe page 266

spicy chicken soup with chili, lime & scallions
Prepare the basic recipe, adding a bunch of scallions, sliced, to the soup just before ladling into bowls.

spicy chicken noodle soup with chili & lime
Prepare the basic recipe, adding 4 oz. vermicelli to the soup with the chicken. Simmer until the noodles are tender, then ladle into bowls.

spicy shrimp soup with chili & lime
Prepare the basic recipe, omitting the chicken and adding 24 deveined, shelled raw tiger shrimp instead. Simmer until the shrimp are pink and cooked through.

spicy tofu soup with chili & lime
Prepare the basic recipe, omitting the chicken and adding 9 oz. cubed silken tofu instead.

spicy fish soup with chili & lime
Prepare the basic recipe, omitting the chicken and adding 2 skinned, cubed 5 oz. salmon fillets instead. Simmer until the fish is just cooked through.

strawberry & chili soup

see base recipe page 269

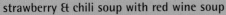

strawberry & chili soup with red wine soup
Prepare the basic recipe, adding 1 cup fruity red wine in place of the
orange juice.

chilled strawberry, pineapple & chili soup
Prepare the basic recipe, using 1 cup pineapple juice in place of the
orange juice.

chilled strawberry, mango & chili soup
Prepare the basic recipe, using half the quantity of strawberries and
replacing them with the flesh of two ripe, peeled and pitted mangoes.

chilled strawberry, apple & chili soup
Prepare the basic recipe, using 1 cup apple juice in place of the orange juice.

chilled strawberry & champagne soup
Prepare the basic recipe, omitting the chili and using 1 cup champagne
or sparkling wine in place of the orange juice.

fish & orange soup

see base recipe page 270

fish & orange soup with chorizo
Prepare the basic recipe, frying 2 oz. diced chorizo sausage with the
onion and garlic.

shrimp & orange soup
Prepare the basic recipe, using 12 oz. shelled, deveined, raw tiger shrimp
in place of the fish.

fish & orange soup with noodles
Prepare the basic recipe, adding 4 oz. vermicelli to the soup with
the fish.

crab & orange soup
Prepare the basic recipe, adding two 6-oz. cans white crabmeat in place
of the fish.

duck & pomegranate soup

see base recipe page 273

duck & orange soup
Prepare the basic recipe, omitting the pomegranates. Stir in 1 teaspoon finely grated orange zest and the juice of 2 oranges, and add a squeeze of lemon juice to taste.

duck & pomegranate soup with red wine
Prepare the basic recipe, using red wine in place of the port.

cream of duck & pomegranate soup
Prepare the basic recipe, stirring 6 tablespoons heavy cream into the soup just before serving.

duck & pomegranate soup with herbs
Prepare the basic recipe, adding 1 bay leaf and 3 fresh thyme sprigs with the stock.

index

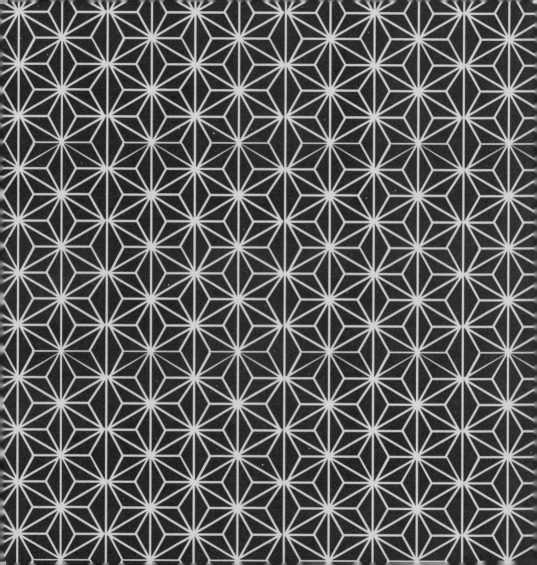